S. Franciscus Xauerius Indiar. Apostolus In Iaponia
Pro fide Lapidatus, Virgis Cæfus, Sagittis Vulneratus,
Non Sine Sanguine, Sed Mirabiliter a Deo Liberatus!

Saint Francis Preaching tothe Japanese
an imaginary portrait

The Catholic Church
in Japan

The Catholic Church in Japan

A Short History

by

Johannes Laures, S. J.

CHARLES E. TUTTLE COMPANY

Rutland, Vermont   Tokyo, Japan

Representatives
For Continental Europe: BOXEBOOKS, INC., Zurich
For the British Isles: PRENTICE-HALL INTERNATIONAL, INC., London
For Australasia: PAUL FLESCH & CO., PTY. LTD., Melbourne

Published by the Charles E. Tuttle Company, Inc.,
of Rutland, Vermont and Tokyo, Japan with
editorial offices at Suido, 1-chome, 2-6
Bunkyo-ku, Tokyo

First edition, Septemper, 1954
Second printing, 1965

IMPRIMI POTEST
Tokyo, die 12ᵃ Martii 1953
Paulus Pfister S. J.
Praepositus Viceprovinciae
Japoniae Societatis Jesu

IMPRIMATUR
Tokyo, die 27ᵃ Junii 1954
Petrus Tatsuo Doi
Archiepiscopus Tokiensis

Printed in Japan

Foreword

The history of the Catholic Church in Japan is perhaps the most tragic and, at the same time, the most thrilling page in the annals of Christianity. The Gospel came rather late to the insular empire, but it came almost simultaneously with the Portuguese merchants who discovered the country.

In 1543 three Portuguese merchants landed on the island of Tanegashima, and only six years later on August 15, 1549, St. Francis Xavier came to the city of Kagoshima as the first Christian missionary. He came with great hopes and high expectations, for he was firmly convinced from all he had heard that the Japanese were the best of all peoples who had been discovered thus far.

It was Xavier who made Japan and her wonderful people known in the West, so much so that he may rightly be considered the real discoverer of Japan. There was perhaps never anyone who loved the Japanese people as much as he loved them, and the commemoration of the fourth centenary of his arrival in Japan has proved that they honor and love him as well. Not only Catholics but also non-Catholics vied in their endeavor to pay homage to the man who had planted the seed of the Gospel in their country and who, at the same time, was filled with love and admiration for its chivalrous people.

Nor were Xavier's expectations ill-founded. The seed he had sown grew rapidly and brought forth abundant fruit. Before forty years had elapsed, Japan numbered no less than 200,000 Christians; after the lapse of another forty years, thousands of glorious martyrs shed their blood for their Divine Lord. For more than 200 years after the great persecution it seemed as if the belief in Christ had entirely disappeared from the hearts of this heroic race. Yet, when the country was again opened to foreign intercourse, the world was startled by the fact that many thousands had preserved the faith in spite of the most cruel, the most systematic and the most relentless of persecutions.

It is true that during the last seventy years the Church did not make the progress one might have expected, but the reasons are easily seen. The leaders of the nation were too absorbed in their endeavor to make up for the loss the country had suffered as a result of an almost complete seclusion of more than two centuries. Unfortunately, they were concerned, in the main, with the adoption of the material culture of the West and the unchristian thought which was taught them by the exponents of modern unbelief. They were ignorant of the fact that Western culture was fundamentally Christian, for it was offered them by men who were themselves no longer Christians.

For this reason and many others there were not many converts for the next seventy-five years, but with the close of the Second World War the situation has changed so completely that a rich harvest of souls can rightly be expected in the years to come. Today Japan is one of the few bright spots in a troubled world, and Catholics in particular are full of hope for the prosperous future of their Church in the Land of the Rising Sun.

Throughout this work first sources have been used, particularly the Jesuit *Annual Letters* both published and unpublished as well as standard works on the Japanese mission.

Those wishing to investigate the subject further are referred to the author's other works, particularly *Kirishitan Bunko,* a complete English bibliography of the Japanese mission, published in 1940 with two supplements dated 1941 and 1951, and *Takayama Ukon and the Beginning of the Church in Japan,* published in Japanese in 1948 and in German, 1954.

The author particularly wishes to thank Father William A. Kaschmitter, M. M., for his assistance and to acknowledge his indebtedness to the late

Foreword

Father Joseph P. Ryan, M. M., who read and revised the manuscript.

CONTENTS

Vain Attempts by the City of Macao;
Faith Preserved; Raids upon the Crypto-
Christians.

The frontispiece, dust-jacket illustration, map on the end papers, and all ornaments used throughout the book are reproduced from one of the earliest books on the Catholic martyrs of Japan, printed in Rome in A.D. 1646—*Fasciculus e Japonicis Floribus, suo adhuc madentibus sanguine, compositus a P. Antonio Francisco Cardim é Societate Jesu . . . Qui Leguitus Flores, hos legite, sic quoniam positi suaves miscentur odores.*

I

Saint Francis Xavier, Apostle of Japan

Kagoshima

The great Apostle of the East, Saint Francis Xavier, had the honor of founding the Catholic Church in Japan. In December, 1547, he met three Japanese at Malacca. Their leader was the young *samurai* from Kagoshima, Yajirô, whose name Japanese scholars now agree upon though contemporary sources call him Angirô or Angerô.

Yajirô told Xavier so many good things about his country that the Saint resolved to bring "this best of all peoples discovered thus far" the Good Tidings of Christ, Our Lord. Yajirô and his two companions were baptized on Pentecost Sunday of the following year and, as prospective catechists, were instructed one year longer that they might obtain a deeper understanding of the Christian religion.

The Catholic Church in Japan

In the spring of 1549, Francis, with Father Cosme de Torres and Brother Fernandez, the three Japanese and two servants, started for Japan. It was a long and adventurous voyage but, in spite of endless trials and hardships, the eight landed at Kagoshima, Yajirô's home town, on August 15.

For Xavier, Kagoshima was to be but an initial stopping-place for he wanted to go to the capital, Kyôto, or Miyako (or Meako) according to Jesuit letters. He wished to see the emperor and convert him or, at any rate, to receive permission to preach in all parts of the empire.

The band of missionaries were received with the utmost courtesy. Shimazu Takahisa, the lord of the place, granted a solemn audience to the Saint, allowing him not only to preach but also to baptize anyone wishing to become a Christian.

When Xavier asked for a ship in which to go to Kyôto, Takahisa agreed but, at the same time, pointed out that the favorable sailing season was over and that it would be advisable to wait for six months. It would have been discourteous for Xavier to insist upon leaving at once although waiting such a long time was certain to be a very trying experience.

He and his European companions began studying the difficult Japanese language while Yajirô preached to his relatives and friends. Very soon his wife, daughter, and a number of other persons asked for baptism. As time went on about 100 persons were received into the Church. Yajirô, moreover, translated into Japanese a catechism which Xavier had composed.

In this way six months passed and again Xavier reminded the prince of his promise to supply a ship for the journey, but Takahisa found other pretexts to show that this journey was too dangerous. As a matter of fact, he wanted to detain the Saint indefinitely in his land, for this seemed to him necessary to attract the Portuguese ships to his ports. Since the material gain of foreign trade was all he was interested in, he was in no hurry to deprive himself of Xavier's presence.

Meanwhile nearly a whole year passed and yet no Portuguese ship dropped anchor in Takahisa's domain. In the summer of 1550 a ship did arrive in Hirado, the principal port of Takahisa's enemy, Matsuura Takanobu. It is easy to understand why the prince of Kagoshima felt greatly disappointed and began to ignore Xavier.

At the beginning of his stay at Kagoshima, Xavier had frequent intercourse with the bonzes and was received rather kindly. Some of the bonzes, particularly Ninshitsu, abbot of the Zen monastery of Fukushôji, became Xavier's intimate

3

friends, and, many years later, one of them, although he did not receive baptism, died as a believer in Jesus.

However, when Xavier made many converts, the bonzes became greatly alarmed and urged Takahisa to expel the foreign preacher. The disappointed prince agreed to this the more readily since his hopes for commercial gain had not materialized. Hence he issued an edict to the effect that under pain of death no one should henceforth receive baptism. Those who had already become Christians, however, were left in peace. Xavier, seeing that his stay in the city was of no further use, left Kagoshima and entrusted the little flock to the care of Yajirô.

Towards Kyôto

Shortly before Shimazu Takahisa issued his prohibition, Xavier had paid a visit to the Portuguese who had landed at Hirado. Now he again went to Hirado and was received with open arms by Matsuura Takanobu, the prince of the place. Takanobu, no less than Takahisa, greatly desired to attract the foreign ships to his harbor, and since he at once realized how high Xavier stood in the eyes of the Portuguese merchants, he considered it wise to treat him with the utmost courtesy.

4

Saint Francis Xavier, Apostle of Japan

Although in his heart he was by no means a friend of the foreign religion, he at once gave Xavier permission to preach and make converts among his subjects. The result was that within a very short time no less than 100 persons were baptized. This great success in so short a time was due also to the zeal and linguistic achievements of Brother Fernandez, who could now preach fairly well in Japanese.

Xavier did not intend to stay long in Hirado but wanted to start for Kyôto before the beginning of winter. He did not ask Matsuura for a ship but left with Brother Fernandez and a Japanese convert of Kagoshima, called Bernardo. They started overland towards the end of October and stopped only at Yamaguchi for any length of time. Here Xavier and particularly Fernandez preached at the crossroads and in the homes of those nobles who invited them. They even preached before the prince of the place, Ôuchi Yoshitaka.

They had very little success and were insulted and ridiculed by both children and adults. Their failure was due to their clumsy Japanese, their exotic appearance and their poor clothes. If Xavier believed that he would impress the Japanese by apostolic poverty, he was badly mistaken. Because of his apparent poverty he and his companions met with contempt and ridicule. Seeing that little could be accomplished under such circumstances, the three left Yamaguchi eight days before Christmas and continued their journey toward Kyôto where they arrived probably about the middle of January, 1551.

If Xavier had failed at Yamaguchi, he failed even more conspicuously in the capital. He had hoped to visit the emperor and to obtain permission to preach wherever he might choose. He did not know that to see the emperor of Japan was the privilege of very few mortals and one quite beyond the reach of a poor foreign preacher of the Gospel. Nor would it have helped him very much if he had been admitted to an audience with the emperor and even been granted the privilege of making converts wherever he pleased.

In those days the emperor, or *tennô*, was but a nominal ruler and had been since the 12th century. He retained the right to grant titles and confer offices but actually had very little authority beyond the confines of his own palace. The *shôgun*, who was nominally to rule the country in the name of the emperor and to be the feudal suzerain of the military clans and actual ruler of Japan, was now but a figurehead. He had been ousted from the capital by his own first minister and at present lived in exile.

The real power was in the hands of the *daimyô,*

or local chieftains, and their power was absolute. The early missionaries later referred to them as kings though, actually, their nearest European feudal counterpart was duke. The *samurai* were the retainers of the *daimyô*. They were the lowest rank of military nobles and corresponded to the feudal knights.

This was the distribution of power when Christianity was first introduced into Japan. The people of Kyôto were scarcely in the proper mood, harassed as they were by fear of impending war, to listen to an odd-looking, poorly clad and somewhat unintelligible preacher of a new religion.

Realizing that nothing could be accomplished for the time being, Xavier left the capital after a short stay of only eleven days. Although his expectations had been disappointed, he had, nevertheless, made two important discoveries. He knew that the emperor had no real power and that the actual rulers of Japan were the local *daimyô*; he, moreover, realized that his failure at Yamaguchi was due, in no small degree, to his humble manner and poor appearance. Being told that the mightiest man in Japan was the *daimyô* of Yamaguchi, he resolved to visit him once more, but this time as an official ambassador of the viceroy of India.

The Catholic Church in Japan

Great Success at Yamaguchi

From Miyako, Xavier returned to Hirado where meanwhile Father Torres had baptized some forty new converts. At once he made preparations for a second visit to Yamaguchi. He had brought with him from Goa an official message from the viceroy of India to the emperor of Japan, in which His Majesty was asked to receive kindly and protect the messengers of the Gospel. The bishop of Goa had entrusted him with a letter of similar contents. The governor of Malacca, Pedro de Silva, a son of the famous Vasco da Gama, had given the Saint a great many precious presents, which he was to offer to the emperor to win his favor. As an audience with the emperor had been impossible, Xavier now resolved to offer both messages and presents to the lord of Yamaguchi. Thus he clothed himself in a garb worthy of an ambassador and started with Brother Fernandez and other companions for Yamaguchi.

This time he met with a most gracious reception. The messages of the viceroy and the bishop, written on fine parchment in beautiful letters, greatly pleased the *daimyô*, and the presents, things never before seen in Japan, aroused his admiration. At once he offered Xavier a large quantity of silver and gold and many other pre-

8

cious things, but Xavier courteously refused to accept them and merely asked for the favor of preaching and making converts. It was willingly granted. He was, moreover, given an old temple as residence.

No sooner had the rumor of the honorable reception of the foreign preacher spread in the city than a great multitude of visitors flocked to Xavier's residence, asked numerous questions about the movements of the stars, eclipses of the sun and the moon and the like. Xavier's clever answers pleased them and greatly enhanced his authority as a scholar. Then the Saint talked of matters of faith and was eagerly heard. It was not long before a good many asked for baptism and within two months about 500 persons were received into the Church. Of this number many were of the higher classes, particularly the *samurai* class. There were even a number of bonzes, among them a great scholar, who had been looking for the truth in various Buddhist sects. The great zeal of these new converts, their charity towards the poor and their attachment to the missionaries filled Xavier with such deep joy that he could not find enough words of praise for these "dear friends".

As may be well understood, Xavier's success aroused the jealousy of the disciples of Buddha,

who by various calumnies endeavored to draw the
people away, although fear of the *daimyô*, Xavier's
protector, kept them from acts of physical violence.
The new converts took it upon themselves not only
to refute the charges against the missionaries but
also to take the offensive and warn the people
against the deceits of the bonzes.

Bungo

After the lapse of about five months Xavier received a personal invitation from Ôtomo Yoshishige, lord of Bungo and later called Ôtomo Sôrin.
This young prince wrote to him that a Portuguese
ship had dropped anchor in one of his ports and
that he wanted to talk over a number of important
things with him. Since Ôtomo was known as a
great friend of the Portuguese, Xavier gladly accepted his invitation and hoped to lead him to the
faith. At once he recalled Father Torres from
Hirado and with three Japanese proceeded to
Bungo, where he was most kindly received by the
daimyô and the Portuguese. He did not succeed
in converting Ôtomo, but his saintly personality
made a deep and lasting impression upon the
young prince. Some twenty-seven years later he
did become a Christian and it was, to no small
extent, a result of this visit.

About Xavier's activity in Bungo we know very

little, but it is certain that he asked for and received permission to preach and make converts. He did make a number of converts, though it is inconceivable that he disputed with the most famous bonzes of the country, as Mendez Pinto, who at that time was in Bungo, would have us believe. Xavier had brought no interpreter with him, nor had he such a command of Japanese that he could have ventured to argue with the first scholars of Japan.

While Xavier was staying in Bungo, Ôuchi Yoshitaka fell victim to a revolt that had broken out at Yamaguchi. Fortunately Father Torres and his companions were unharmed, due to the protection of Xavier's noble friend, Naitô Takaharu. Almost simultaneously with Father Torres' messenger, a delegation of the rebels called on Ôtomo and offered his younger brother, Haruhide, the position of the late Ôuchi as lord of Yamaguchi and the rest of his vast domain. With the approval of his elder brother, Haruhide accepted the offer and promised to protect the Fathers and favor Christianity. From then on he called himself Ôuchi Yoshinaga.

Return to India

Ôtomo Yoshishige greatly desired to keep Xavier in Bungo, but did not succeed. For more

The Catholic Church in Japan

than two years the Saint had received no news
from India, and so he felt that his obligations as
superior of the Indian mission imperatively demanded his presence in that country. He wanted
to stay there only for a short time so as to put
things in order and immediately return to Japan
with a many new workers. His casual meeting
with his friend, Diogo Pereira, on Sancian brought
about a change of plan,

Pereira, having just returned from China, told
Francis of the terrible sufferings of his countrymen in Chinese prisons, where they had been
thrown for smuggling themselves into the country
against the most severe prohibition of the emperor.
Xavier, moved to pity for these unfortunates, proposed that Pereira should go as ambassador of the
viceroy of India to the court of Peking to relieve
his countrymen and that he himself would accompany him to establish a mission in the Chinese
empire. If the Church could attract the Chinese
people, Xavier was convinced that the Japanese
would follow their example, since China ranked
so high in the eyes of the Japanese. Thus by converting China Xavier hoped to accelerate the conversion of Japan.

It is a well-known fact that Xavier's plans were
frustrated because of the jealousy of the governor
of Malacca. Yet he landed on the island of San-

cian, hoping against hope that some courageous boatman would smuggle him into forbidden China. He found none. The frustration of his cherished hope together with the superhuman privations on that desert island broke Xavier's health. He was seized with a deadly fever and died there, at the very gates of China, on December 3, 1552.

St. Francis Xavier is rightly called the Apostle of Japan. He was the first missionary to introduce Christianity into the insular empire. He had supplied it with first-class workers, had founded four churches and last but not least had won for the nascent Church the friendship of two powerful princes. Although his expectations and mass conversions were not realized and he had baptized no more than about one thousand souls, he considered his journey to Japan a great success. He was convinced that the Christian faith would soon strike deep roots in the hearts of the Japanese people and that they would give their lives for their faith. Hence he firmly believed that this wonderful people deserved to have the very best missionaries he could find among his brethren. The glorious history of the martyr Church of Japan is justification of his admiration for the marvellous gifts of this chivalrous people.

II

Slow Progress

New Workers

After Xavier's return to India Father Torres remained the only priest in Japan. He and Brother Fernandez were working with great zeal and success at Yamaguchi. After Ôtomo Haruhide, later called Ôuchi Yoshinaga, had taken over the claims of the late Ôuchi Yoshitaka, peace and order were restored at Yamaguchi, and since the new *daimyô* showed himself a protector of the Christians, the work of evangelization proceeded satisfactorily. The piece of land which Ôuchi Yoshitaka had donated to the Fathers had been confiscated during the rebellion in 1551, but was restored the following year. Thus a new church and a priest's house could again be erected.

Xavier had been busy with his Chinese project but he by no means forgot Japan. When he set

out for China he sent three of his brethren to Japan:
Father Balthasar Gago and the lay-brothers Duarte
da Silva and Pedro de Alcaçova. They arrived at
Kagoshima on August 14, 1552. Shimazu Takahisa, who had compelled Xavier to leave, had
evidently changed his hostile attitude, for he received the three newcomers with great courtesy.
If we may trust Alcaçova's report (Goa, 1554),
the number of Christians at Kagoshima had increased to about 500 souls, yet this seems scarcely
credible in view of the fact that baptism had been
prohibited under a death penalty and that Yajirô
had been ousted by the bonzes. Be this as it may,
the three newcomers, knowing very little Japanese,
could do nothing for these abandoned Christians
and, moreover, had received strict orders to proceed immediately to Bungo. So they stayed only
two weeks at Kagoshima and started for Bungo.

When Ôtomo learned of their arrival he immediately assigned them living quarters. The following day they were received in audience and
offered the prince a letter and presents from the
viceroy of India. Ôtomo was greatly pleased and
daily sent food to their house. When Father
Torres heard of the arrival of the three he dispatched Brother Fernandez to Bungo to serve as
interpreter. He was assigned to translate the
viceroy's letter for Ôtomo and to speak to him

about the "things of God". Accordingly all four missionaries visited the prince, and Brother Fernandez discharged his mission. About Ôtomo's reaction to the Brother's address on the "things of God" we are not informed, but we know that Father Gago, five days later and various times afterwards, called on the *daimyô* to convert him to the Christian religion. Among other things he read, in Ôtomo's presence, a *rômaji* text of the decalogue but could not explain the exact sense of the various commandments, since he didn't know enough Japanese. As a result, Ôtomo (believing that the fifth commandment, "Thou shalt not kill," forbade killing anyone under any circumstances) wondered how a vigorous government was possible if a criminal could not lawfully be executed.

Father Gago did not succeed in converting the prince, who gave only evasive answers, but nevertheless expressed a genuine desire to see the Christian religion spread among his subjects. He greatly regretted that there were not as yet many Christians in Bungo, whereas at Yamaguchi there was already a numerous flock of believers. Hence he urged the missionaries to remain in Bungo. Father Gago thereupon replied that they had received orders first to go to Yamaguchi and added that before there could be a question of spreading the faith in Bungo it was indispensible that freedom of preaching and baptizing should be granted by the lord of the land. Ôtomo declared himself at once ready to grant this request, but Gago asked him to wait until their return from Yamaguchi. Finally Ôtomo gave them permission to leave. Alcaçova left Bungo very soon and Silva a few days later, but Gago and Fernandez remained until shortly before Christmas.

At Christmas all the Fathers and Brothers met at Yamaguchi. The presence of so many made it possible to celebrate this feast with greater solemnity than had been done in the previous year. Thus the Japanese Christians to their great satisfaction for the first time attended a High Mass. The newcomers were deeply impressed by the piety and charity of the Christians.

After the lapse of about one month Father Torres gave Father Gago and the four Brothers their assignments. All had agreed that Brother Alcaçova should return to India to report on the state of the mission and to plead for more helpers; Brother Silva was to remain with Father Torres at Yamaguchi, whereas Father Gago and Brother Fernandez were to start work in Bungo. Alcaçova accompanied Gago and Fernandez to Bungo whence he was to proceed to Hirado to embark for India. The three reached Bungo on February 4, 1553.

Brother Alcaçova received a letter from Ôtomo

for the viceroy of India and a few days later went alone to Hirado where he remained until October 18. During this long stay he several times visited the *daimyô,* Matsuura Takanobu, who received him with exquisite courtesy. The clever prince expressed an ardent desire to have priests in his land and to see the Christian faith spread among his subjects. He even told the good Brother that in his heart he himself was almost a Christian. While Alcaçova was in Hirado, Father Gago came over from Bungo for a short visit of two weeks. He had the satisfaction of converting many souls and among them three of the principal noblemen, who were near relatives of Matsuura. One of the three was Koteda Saemon (Dom Antonio) and another was Saemon's younger brother, Ichibu Kageyu (Dom João). Dom Antonio was to become the fearless protagonist and protector of the faith in Hirado. His sons sacrificed everything for the sake of their faith and went into exile in 1599, and a grandson of his was to be a glorious martyr.

Before his departure Brother Alcaçova received a letter from Matsuura for the viceroy of India in which the prince urged that priests be sent to his land. Alcaçova on his way home learned of Xavier's death on Sancian, but when he arrived there the earthly remains of the Saint had already been taken to Malacca. In that city he saw Xavier's body and

19

accompanied it to Goa which he reached on March 16, 1554.

In the same year Brother Alcaçova sent a report to Portugal which deserves special interest. It was about the number of Christians in Japan. We have already expressed grave doubts about the trustworthiness of the figure he gives for Kagoshima. It is unthinkable that at his arrival there should have been 500 Christians at Kagoshima or even in the entire province of Satsuma. Nor do we know of any attempt to resume missionary work in Shimazu's domain between the Brother's arrival in Japan and the year of the dispatch of his letter to Portugal. At first sight it would seem also that the figure he gives for Bungo, 600 to 700 souls, is greatly exaggerated. When he arrived in that province there were scarcely any Christians in Ôtomo's domain, as we learn from the latter's own words. Yet it must be remembered that before Brother Alcaçova left Japan Father Gago and Brother Fernandez had been working with great zeal in Bungo and might well have baptized 600 or 700 persons. The figures given for Yamaguchi, 1,500, and Hirado, 200, may safely be taken at their face value.

Gago's Activity in Hirado and Bungo

As has been stated, Father Gago visited Hirado

in 1553 and during a brief stay of two weeks made a number of converts, particularly three near relatives of the *daimyô*. In 1555 he was again in Hirado and remained there for more than six months. At the beginning of September, Matsuura Takanobu donated a piece of land for a Christian cemetery. The large cross of the new burial place was dedicated on September 14, 1555. This time Gago was accompanied by Brother Fernandez and a converted bonze called Paul of whom more will be said later. Since both Brother Fernandez and Paul were very zealous and skilful missionaries, the number of conversions must have been considerable. According to Father Gago's report there were nearly 500 Christians in Hirado on September 23, 1555, that is at the beginning of his stay in that year, whereas Brother Alcaçova's letter of the preceding year gives only 200.

In Bungo also, Gago and Fernandez vigorously endeavored to make converts. A rebellion shortly after their arrival compelled Ôtomo to fortify himself in his castle. Thus the missionaries could not expect protection from him but they feared for his safety. To console the harassed *daimyô,* Gago sent Fernandez to the castle to tell Ôtomo that he should trust in the Lord's help and that he himself would pray for him. Ôtomo greatly appreciated this act of charity and thanked the Father for his thoughtfulness. Happily the rebellion was soon crushed and order restored.

A good number of baptisms was the result of Father Gago's and Brother Fernandez' endeavor, but opposition on the part of the bonzes was also very strong. They spread all kinds of calumnies about the missionaries and even charged them with cannibalism. They threw stones at their house. Ôtomo put guards around it and threatened to punish anyone who would dare insult or molest the foreign preachers. As a result, open insults ceased and the number of converts rose from day to day. Ôtomo had donated a piece of land, and at once Gago began the construction of a chapel and a priest's house. On July 22, 1553, a large cross was erected with appropriate ceremonies, which drew large crowds of visitors and enhanced the self-consciousness of the Christians. Gago and his companion did not confine their activity to the capital but also made excursions to the neighboring towns and villages. At Kutami, they gathered a rich harvest of souls.

While Father Gago was thus working in Bungo he received the visit of a young and wealthy Portuguese, Luis d'Almeida. He was a merchant and had also some knowledge in surgery but now resolved to devote his life to the Japanese mission. He landed at Hirado, probably in 1554, and thence went to Bungo to meet Father Gago and consult with him about his future life. When the Father told him how many mothers killed their children for economic reasons, he was moved to deep compassion and offered to erect a foundling home where children might be nursed and raised. The governor of Funai (now Ôita) approved of the idea. Almeida spent 1,000 *cruzados* in erecting and equipping a building and he personally took charge. Ôtomo gave orders to hand over the unwanted children to the missionaries and to provide nurses to look after them. The foundling home served also as a place of refuge for poor Christians. Not much later Almeida founded a hospital. Surgery being unknown in Japan, Almeida himself treated surgical cases and trained Japanese helpers in surgery, which was thus introduced into Japan.

The Japanese were greatly impressed by this charitable work and many who had been cured of their diseases or received financial help asked for baptism. As a result the number of Christians rose within two years to about 2,000. The fact, however, that nearly all of them belonged to the lower classes or were moved to accept baptism out of gratitude for benefits received was a stumbling block to the higher classes and kept them aloof. They believed that the Christian religion was the faith of the poor and the sick. Thus the works of charity, far from attracting the people to the Church, as usually happens, had exactly the opposite effect.

Yamaguchi

Father Torres and Brother Silva worked with great zeal and remarkable success at Yamaguchi. Here it was above all their charitable help during a famine in 1554 which led many to the faith. A number of notable conversions took place. Watanabe Torozaemon, a valiant *samurai* of Sue Harukata, who had invited Ôtomo Haruhide to succeed the late Ôuchi Yoshitaka, became a fervent Christian and a fearless defender of the faith. About the same time two learned bonzes, Kyozen and Senyô, of the famous monastery of Tônomine, in the province of Yamato, came to Yamaguchi to study the Christian religion. Both of them were well versed in the Japanese sects and, moreover, Kyozen was an excellent physician. Having listened to the sermons for some time they resolved their doubts and finally received baptism. Kyozen was christened Paul and Senyô, Barnabas. This happened in 1554. In the following year Xavier's friend, Naitô Takaharu, was baptized with his two sons. The ex-bonze, Paul, went with Gago and Fernandez to Hirado in 1555 and displayed extraordinary zeal as preacher and catechist.

Lorenzo at Hieizan

While Xavier had tried in vain to establish a mission at Kyôto, Father Torres never gave up hope of accomplishing what his master had failed to realize and was eagerly looking for an opportunity to resume Xavier's project. The conversion of the two bonzes, Paul and Barnabas, brought him one step nearer to its execution. Having talked over the matter with them, he learned that without the approval of Hieizan, the famous Tendai monastery at Sakamoto, it was impossible to preach a new religion in the capital. Consequently it was decided that Lorenzo, the almost blind bard whom Xavier had baptized at Yamaguchi, should go with Barnabas to Hieizan to obtain the desired approval. Paul gave them a letter of introduction to his friend, Daizenbô, a very influential bonze at Hieizan, that by his good offices they might obtain an interview with the head-bonze, Shinkai.

Daizenbô received the two courteously but was unwilling to do anything for them. He advised Lorenzo to try by himself to meet Shinkai. Although he had not received a letter of introduction, Lorenzo cleverly managed to be admitted to Shinkai. The kindly old man even listened to Lorenzo's sermon and was greatly pleased with it, but being half deaf and living already in retirement, he advised Lorenzo to call once more on Daizenbô so as to obtain Hieizan's approval. Daizenbô was not only surprised but also greatly embarrassed at Lorenzo's return and, in order to get rid of him without appearing discourteous, he advised him to return to Kyûshû and secure a letter of introduction to the abbot of Hieizan from the *daimyô* of Yamaguchi, since the abbot had formerly resided in that city and was a favorite of the *daimyô*. Lorenzo and Barnabas were put off indefinitely and returned to Kyûshû. They had started from Yamaguchi but, meanwhile, Father Torres had been compelled to flee to Bungo.

Expulsion from Yamaguchi

Ôtomo Haruhide had been raised to the daimyate by the rebel, Sue Harukata, and was little more than his puppet. Nor had he the backing of his people, the majority of whom—particularly the nobility—were opposed to the regime of the traitor, Sue Harukata. Before Ôuchi Yoshitake took his own life through *harakiri* in 1551, he is said to have written to Môri Motonari, his faithful ally from the province of Aki, extracting a promise to avenge his death.

Motonari, faithful to this request, began making plans against Sue Harukata and Ôuchi Yoshinaga as early as 1553. He obtained an imperial order to punish them and in 1554 began war against them. Victory followed victory and in the spring of 1556 Yoshinaga was forced to leave Yamaguchi. His opponents burned several parts of the city including the church and the priest's house. The Christians urged Father Torres to flee to Bungo which he did in May, 1556.

Soon after, Lorenzo and Barnabas returned from Gokinai (the five provinces around the capital: Yamashiro, Yamato, Kawachi, Settsu and Izumi) and reported the failure of their mission. Far from being discouraged, Father Torres advised Lorenzo to obtain the letter of introduction to the head bonze of Hieizan from Ôuchi Yoshinaga, who was still holding out against Motonari and, for the time being, seemed to be winning. Consequently in the spring of 1557 the Christians invited Father Torres to return to Yamaguchi.

The Father was willing to comply with their wishes but upon Yoshinaga's advice he saw that it would be wiser to wait and see the eventual outcome of the struggle. Very soon he received the sad news that Yamaguchi was again the enemy's and that Ôuchi Yoshinaga had lost his life.

Many of the leading Christians, particularly the Christian *samurai,* who had sided with Yoshinaga, had to flee to escape Motonari's revenge. Thus only about 300 Christians remained in the ravaged city.

27

The Catholic Church in Japan

The church property was seized by the enemies but was soon recovered by a court decision. Thereupon the Christians built another church, but it was destroyed by Motonari, who confiscated the land. As a staunch Buddhist he was very hostile to the Christian religion and as long as he lived no priest or catechist was allowed to visit the abandoned flock. Even after Motonari's death in 1571, it was fifteen years before Yamaguchi again received a residing priest and then only for one year. This most favored church of Saint Francis Xavier had from the very beginning experienced hard times but neverless flourished from 1551 to 1557. Having lost their pastor in 1556, the harassed Christians were, for the most part, left to themselves but in spite of all trials and persecutions they kept the faith, as shall be seen.

Melchior Nunez Barreto's Visit

Alcaçova's report on the Japanese mission, particularly the favorable disposition of the *daimyô* of Bungo and Hirado, made such an impression of the provincial of India, Father Melchior Nunez Barreto, that he resolved to go to Japan himself. Although he had been hesitating, in view of his heavy responsibilities as provincial of India, all doubts were dispersed by the heroic resolution of the wealthy merchant and adventurer, Fernão

Mendez Pinto, to join the Society of Jesus and to devote the rest of his life to the Church of Japan. Father Barreto resolved to accompany Pinto to Japan but advised him to postpone his entry into the Society and to fulfil first the mission of an ambassador of the viceroy of India to the court of the *daimyô* of Bungo, who had sent his ambassador to Goa in 1551.

Nunez Barreto left Goa on April 1, 1554, but did not arrive in Bungo until July, 1556. He was shipwrecked, harassed by pirates and, because of alarming reports from India, was undecided whether to continue his journey. On the island of Lampacau off the coast of China he met Duarte da Gama, who had just returned from Japan and told him that the Japanese Christians awaited him. He had brought with him a letter from Matsuura Takanobu of Hirado, who urgently asked for priests and said that he himself was in his heart almost a Christian. Another letter from Luis d'Almeida urged Nunez Barreto to come to Japan that he might consult with him about the future. Together with his letter Almeida sent 2,000 *cruzados* to help Nunez in his needs during his voyage. Now all doubts disappeared and the Provincial continued his journey to Japan. Together with him travelled Father Gaspar Vilela, three brothers and three orphan children. Shortly before their arrival Father Torres and Brother Fernandez had fled from Yamaguchi so that Nunez Barreto found the entire missionary staff assembled in Bungo in July, 1556.

Pinto discharged his duties as ambassador and then joined the Society of Jesus as a lay-brother. Nunez Barreto tried very hard to convert Ôtomo to the Christian faith but failed. These are the reasons according to Nunez Barreto: the *daimyô* was afraid that his conversion might lead to rebellion; he was too deeply immerged in the vices of the flesh and was, moreover, an ardent adept of Zen Buddhism. Having failed to convert the prince, Nunez Barreto proposed a disputation with the bonzes. Ôtomo apparently agreed but nothing came of it. A very real reason for Nunez Barreto's failure was the troubled state of the capital as a result of which Ôtomo had to change his residence to the strong fortress of Usuki.

Nunez stayed only about four months in Japan. During this time he composed a book, which Lorenzo translated into Japanese and which did good service in the early days of the mission in Kyôto in 1559. Accompanied by Brother Fernandez, Nunez Barreto visited the churches of Bungo and was greatly edified by the piety of the Christians. Yet the strain of the missionary life was too much for his health. The strange Japanese food and the primitive bedding had such an effect on his delicate health that he fell ill. He himself more than anyone else clearly realized that Japan was not for him and as soon as he had recovered sufficiently he resolved to return to India where, moreover, his presence was greatly needed. Pinto, who also found life in the Society too hard, was dismissed from the order and returned to India together with the provincial in November, 1556.

Nunez Barreto's most valuable service to the Japanese mission was the introduction of Almeida into the Society of Jesus. This generous and remarkable man was to do excellent work as a doctor, a preacher and catechist and, for a very short time, a priest. It was he who converted the first *daimyô*, Ômura Sumitada, to the Christian religion, and it was due to his skilful negotiations and charitable help that missions were opened on the Gotô Archipelago, in Arima and in Amakusa. He to a very great extent financed the various charitable institutions in Bungo, about which more will be said hereafter, and by donating the rest of his substantial fortune to his order he greatly relieved the financial strain on the Fathers.

Missionary Work: 1556-1559

The main work was carried on in Bungo.

The Catholic Church in Japan

Although there was some progress it was very moderate. In Hirado there were mass conversions but in the end the hostility of the bonzes and of the *daimyô* himself threatened the Church with complete destruction. The only new mission established was at Hakata but in the following year the Fathers were compelled to leave the city. The abandoned Christians of Yamaguchi suffered greatly under the tyranny of Môri Motonari and could not even be visited by the missionaries. In 1559 the only safe place for the Fathers was Bungo where they had fled from Hirado and Hakata. It was the most critical moment in the history of the Japanese mission. All that had been accomplished seemed lost, and the future looked very dark indeed. The fact that the Fathers did not lose courage but even set out for new projects shows their undaunted courage and generous zeal.

When in June, 1556, Father Torres fled to Bungo from Yamaguchi the number of faithful had risen to about 2,000. During the next twenty years there was scarcely any increase whatever. One of the reasons for this lack of success was the fact that nearly all converts came from the lower ranks. Another reason which particularly kept the *samurai* class from joining the Church was Ôtomo's unwillingness to receive baptism. This is surprising as he showed the highest respect for the

Fathers, showered his favors on them, protected and defended them against their enemies and helped them in every possible way to make converts.

It has been said above that in 1555 Almeida established a foundling home and not much later a hospital as well in the capital of Bungo. At all events, in 1557 there was a hospital at Funai with two sections, one for lepers and other incurables and another for curable diseases. In this second section there was also a department for surgical cases, of which Almeida himself took care. As a result of the large number of successful cures the reputation of this hospital spread far and wide so that it reached not only Kyôto but even the distant provinces of northeastern Japan. From these remote regions there came so many bonzes, *samurai* and other distinguished people to be cured of their diseases that the hospital could not possibly accommodate so many applicants. Thus, as early as 1559, a second and much larger hospital was built. Whereas the older institution in the main had treated people of the lower classes, the new hospital was meant to serve the needs of people of higher rank.

Apart from Japanese laymen, a number of Jesuit Brothers as well were taught medicine and surgery by Almeida, whereas all Fathers and

Brothers devoted themselves to the nursing and ministry of the patients. Internal diseases had, from the very beginning, been treated in the main by Japanese and Chinese laymen, one of whom joined the Society of Jesus and eventually took charge of the internal section. Almeida was so successful in training surgical assistants that as early as 1561 he could hand over the surgical section to them and devote himself entirely to the direct apostolate.

The means for constructing and supporting these hospitals came from various sources. Almeida himself paid for the foundling home and spent the rest of his large fortune, in as far as he did not devote it to the support of the missionaries, for hospitals and charitable works. Another part of the money was contributed by Portuguese merchants who had come to Bungo to be cured of their diseases. Ôtomo himself granted an annual sum of from 300 to 500 *cruzados*, although during the first year his treasurer kept the money for himself. Finally the Misericordia Brotherhood collected funds in the form of many small gifts from the Christians.

Apart from charitable work the missionaries very soon engaged in education as well. They established a school for boys who were to be future catechists and preachers. There were 15 students in 1562, partly Japanese and partly Chinese. Reading, writing, Christian doctrine and music were taught.

Although tangible success in the number of converts was very slight in Bungo, it was, nevertheless, the only place where the Fathers could work undisturbed and where they always found refuge and hospitality when they had been expelled from other places.

Since Xavier's visit Matsuura Takanobu had diligently fostered the friendship of the missionaries, had repeatedly asked for priests and even declared that he himself was almost a Christian. The missionaries for a long time honestly believed that he was their friend. Actually it was only craft. He greatly desired to draw the Portuguese ships to his port because of the great economic gain to his land. Hirado had a very good harbor and, consequently, the Portuguese merchants eventually preferred it to all other ports of Kyûshû. When Matsuura became aware of this he believed that the time had come when he could throw off the mask and withdraw his favor from the missionaries. Until then he had simulated benevolence and even zeal for the Christian religion, although in his heart he was its bitter enemy.

Before leaving Japan Father Nunez Barreto had appointed Father Gago and Brother Silva to the

The Catholic Church in Japan

mission of Hirado, which for the first time was to have resident missionaries. In 1558 Hirado had a church. Father Gago and Brother Silva worked peacefully and successfully for more than a year. In September, 1557, two Portuguese ships arrived at Hirado harbor, and the crew asked Father Torres for another priest since Father Gago was too much occupied with converting. Thereupon Father Vilela was sent to Hirado. The two priests availed themselves of the presence of the Portuguese and impressed the Japanese with processions and solemn ceremonies. When the Portuguese had left the city Father Gago received orders to establish a mission in the city of Hakata, where previously Ôtomo had donated a piece of land. Father Vilela was to take Gago's place in Hirado.

Meanwhile the progress of the mission had stirred up the jealousy of the bonzes which they showed by various acts of violence and hostility. Dom Antonio, realizing that evangelical work was becoming more and more difficult in Hirado, invited Father Vilela to preach to his subjects on the island of Takushima. The Father gathered a rich harvest, for within a short time no less than 600 baptisms were administered. Encouraged by this success, Dom Antonio resolved to eradicate paganism and burned a good many temples and pagan images. The result was a great stir among the bonzes, one of whom had a great following and began to speak most violently against the Christians. Stirred up by his invectives, three ruffians cut down the cross in the cemetery at Hirado and the bonzes threatened to destroy the church also. Dom Antonio protested so vigorously that they did not venture to carry out their threat. He moreover called upon Matsuura to protect the Christians and to punish the three young men who had profaned the cross. Matsuura promised to comply with this request but did nothing to stop the anti-Christian agitation. On the contrary, he soon after begged Father Vilela with kindly words to withdraw for a time and to return to Bungo. This occurred in 1558.

Vilela honestly believed that Matsuura regretted his withdrawal because he was unable to force his will upon the bonzes, but the fact is that the clever prince, no less than the bonzes, greatly rejoiced in getting rid of the priest whose religion he hated. After Father Vilela had left the city the bonzes again attempted to destroy the church but because of Dom Antonio's opposition did not succeed. In the following year, however, the church fell a victim to their hatred.

It soon became evident that Matsuura wanted to have the missionaries permanently exiled from his land, for when the Christians invited Father Gago to Hirado the prince would not allow him to live in the city, nor even permit the Fathers to travel through his domain. After Gago's departure nine leading Christians were called upon to deny their faith, which they refused to do. During the night they fled to Bungo, but in the great hurry some of them were unable to take their wives and children with them. After their arrival in Bungo they implored Ôtomo's help in behalf of their relatives. Thereupon Ôtomo urged Matsuura to send them to Bungo, which he did. It was six years before the mission in Hirado could be re-established. Only on Dom Antonio's islands were the Christians living in peace; the work of evangelization went on and the churches were left intact.

The Christians of Hirado soon erected another cross and said their prayers before it every morning and evening. A Christian servant girl was warned by her master that he would kill her if she did not stop visiting the cross. Seeing nothing unlawful in saying her prayers before the cross, she did not heed her master's threat and continued her pious visits. When one evening she returned from the cross her master in a fit of anger cut off her head. She was the first martyr of the Church of Japan. According to the local tradition her Christian name was Mary.

Môri Motonari, having destroyed Ôuchi Yoshinaga, Ôtomo's younger brother, became engaged in a fierce struggle with the powerful lord of Bungo. Although Ôtomo could not recover Yoshinaga's entire fief, he took from Motonari the two provinces of Buzen and Chikuzen. Wishing to spread Christianity in his new domain, Ôtomo donated a piece of land in the city of Hakata, the capital of Chikuzen. In 1557 Father Gago left Hirado to take possession of the land, but soon returned to Bungo to have the donation formally confirmed by Ôtomo. In the spring of 1558 he was back at Hakata and began preaching. Many came to listen to his sermons but only a few received baptism. His small congregation of neophytes was strengthened by a number of old Christians from Yamaguchi.

After a peaceful year a great upheaval occurred on Easter Monday in 1559. An armed band of 2,000 ruffians appeared at the gates of the city and complained that they had been unjustly expelled from their property by the governor of the "king of Bungo". As they were denied entrance into the city they took the gate by force and committed acts of great violence. Father Gago and Brother Fernandez fled to a ship but were caught by bandits, robbed of all they had and threatened with death. For three months they were kept in custody and trembled for their lives. Finally they were delivered by a Christian who had a friend among the bandits, and were sent safe and sound to Bungo.

The Catholic Church in Japan

As a result of the terrible ordeal Gago suffered a nervous breakdown, lost all interest in the mission and had to be sent back to India in 1561. In 1559 work was resumed at Hakata, and two years later the city had a new church, but as no priest could permanently reside there, this was scarcely progress.

Thus in the spring of 1559 all the Fathers and Brothers were in Bungo with shattered hopes and with little prospect of resuming work in the two flourishing missions of Yamaguchi and Hirado. Bungo was the only safe place but despite the most heroic efforts the number of Christians was small nor were there any prospects of a change for the better as long as Ôtomo declined to become a Christian. Despite such gloomy prospects Father Torres was by no means discouraged.

III

Foundation of a Mission in Gokinai

Father Vilela and Lorenzo at Hieizan

It will be recalled how the bonze, Daizenbô, had put off Lorenzo in 1556 by advising him to secure a letter of introduction from Ôuchi Yoshinaga of Yamaguchi so as to be admitted in audience with the head bonze of Hieizan. When Lorenzo returned from Gokinai Father Torres had fled from Yamaguchi because of Môri Motonari's victories over Yoshinaga. The latter, nevertheless, held out for almost another year, and so Torres sent Lorenzo to him to receive the desired letter for the abbot of Hieizan. On his visit to Hieizan, Lorenzo had been received most kindly by the retired bonze, Shinkai, who showed a keen interest in the Christian religion. Father Torres did not fail to foster Shinkai's friendship and sent him Christian literature that he might penetrate deeper into the Christian doctrine. Shinkai was greatly pleased with what he read about this new religion and requested Father Torres to come himself or send someone else to instruct and baptize him. The reason Father Torres had not complied with this request was simply the fact that no priest was available. But now, when the three Fathers were reduced to forced idleness, it became possible to send a priest to Gokinai, and Father Torres eagerly seized the opportunity to carry out this long cherished project.

Of the three priests only Father Vilela seemed eligible for the difficult enterprise. He was young and strong, good-looking and of amiable manners. He had sufficient command of the language and, moreover, a burning zeal and tenacious endurance. Gago was incapable and also unwilling to take upon himself such a heavy burden after his nervous collapse at Hakata, and Torres was an old man and bound by the duties of his office as superior of the mission to stay in Kyûshû. Father Vilela's companions were Lorenzo and Damian. Lorenzo though greatly handicapped by poor eyesight and ugly features was, nevertheless, a remarkable man because of his extraordinary sagacity and command of the language. Damian was excellent as a catechist and a preacher. Both Lorenzo and Damian later joined the Society of Jesus as lay-brothers and worked zealously and successfully for the spread of the Gospel.

By order of Father Torres, Vilela and his companions were to call at Hieizan to satisfy Shinkai's craving for the Christian truth and to obtain permission to establish a mission in the capital. When they arrived they learned that Shinkai had died as a believer in Christ. Daizenbô, whom they visited, was kind enough but uncompromising. The result was that it proved impossible to obtain Hieizan's approval for the planned mission. Thus Vilela resolved to try by himself to establish a church in Kyôto. He arrived there about the beginning of November, 1559.

It is almost incredible with what difficulties he was faced during the first six months. An old Buddhist nun of Sakamoto had given him a letter of introduction to one of her male relatives asking that the strangers might be lodged in his home. He granted the request only on condition that Father Vilela should not preach or leave the house. Even so the good Father had to move out after about two weeks.

In spite of unspeakable hardships, vexations and molestations Vilela was greatly helped by a kind bonze, Yengennan, to whom he had been introduced, by letter, by a Christian doctor, Paul Yesan of Sakai. Through the good offices of this bonze, the Father was admitted to an audience with the *shôgun,* Yoshiteru. The result was that from now on many visitors came to his residence and asked many questions. Simultaneously, however, the jealousy of the bonzes was stirred up with the result that Vilela had to change lodgings four times within six months. Nobody was willing to expose himself to the boycotting of his customers or to the rage of the disciples of Buddha. In spite of all opposition about 100 persons were baptized in these six months.

In June, 1560, Father Vilela managed to buy a house of his own and to open a modest chapel, yet the enemies bombarded his residence with stones day and night. To put an end to these molestations the Father secured a letter of protection from the *shôgun* which he posted at the entrance of the church. Now open insults ceased but the most fabulous calumnies were circulated. Vilela was charged with cannibalism; the Christian religion, with causing disorder and calamity at both Yamaguchi and Hakata.

Since these calumnies did not make much impression upon the fearless missionary, the enemies tried to oust him from the capital. The bonzes induced Matsunaga Hisahide, the most powerful man in Gokinai, to spread the rumor that the *shôgun* had issued an order to the effect that Vilela was to be expelled from the capital. Matsunaga, through a hypocritical friend of the missionaries, advised them to yield to the storm and leave the city of their own account before the promulgation of the *shôgun's* ordinance. Vilela believed this bluff but assigned Lorenzo to clear up the matter. Lorenzo fulfilled this mission so cleverly and successfully that the whole plot was found to be nothing but an intrigue of Matsunaga, who played innocent so as to extricate himself from the awkward situation. Vilela was able not only to return to the capital but received an even more favorable letter of protection from the *shôgun*.

Not having succeeded in expelling the missionaries, the bonzes now stirred up the people to boycott Father Vilela's preaching. They succeeded only too well. Thereupon he resolved to ride out the storm for the time being and to establish a mission in the great commercial metropolis of Sakai. Xavier on his visit to Kyôto had stopped in the home of the wealthy merchant, Hibiya Ryôkei Kudô of Sakai. Although none of Kudô's family was baptized at that time, his son Fukuda had not forgotten Xavier's visit. Having learned of Father Vilela's presence at Kyôto he begged him to open a mission. Simultaneously he addressed a letter to Father Torres to the same effect. Thereupon Torres ordered Vilela to comply with Fukuda's request and proceed to Sakai, since, after all, he could make very little progress in the capital.

Father Vilela left for Sakai in the summer of 1561 and stayed there until September, 1562. During this time he baptized about forty citizens of Sakai and a somewhat greater number of visitors and merchants from elsewhere. Fukuda extended him the most cordial hospitality from the very beginning and had his children baptized. In 1563 he himself received baptism and became the champion and protector of the Church. For more than eighteen years his house served as church for the small congregation of the city. Father Vilela had come to Gokinai without a Mass kit, evidently because he was not sure of the success of his mission. He was now able to say Mass for the first time after the lapse of three years and a half.

It seems almost providential that Father Vilela left Kyôto in 1561, for scarcely had he gone when civil war broke out in the capital and lasted for more than a year. For this reason the Father had to stay at Sakai much longer than he had originally intended. He nevertheless managed to send Lorenzo to Kyôto to visit the Christians and was gladdened by the good news that they had not only kept the faith but had also greatly edified the non-Christians by their works of charity.

After the end of the civil war Father Vilela

returned to the capital. On September 8, he said the first Mass. Because of the hostile propaganda of the bonzes very few non-Christians listened to his sermons and so he availed himself of the stalemate to impart to his faithful a deeper knowledge of the faith. Even so the enemies did not acquiesce and worked out another scheme to oust the foreign preacher from the capital.

As we have seen Father Vilela had obtained a letter of protection from the *shôgun*, Yoshiteru. A similar favor had been granted by the *shôgun's* first minister, Miyoshi Chôkei. Even Miyoshi's Minister of Justice, Matsunaga Hisahide, who by no means was a friend of the foreign religion, could not help extending his protection to the missionaries seeing that they were favored by his superiors. When the bonzes urged him to exile the Father he replied that he could not do so without a formal trial by the evidence of which it would become clear that the Christian religion was immoral and dangerous for the safety of the city. To be sure of the outcome of the trial he appointed as judges two scholars, Yûki and Kiyohara, sworn enemies of the Christian religion. If the two were to find that Christianity was bad, which they undoubtedly would, the Father was to be expelled and his church to be confiscated.

Matsunaga's retainer, Takayama Hida-no-

The Catholic Church in Japan

Kami, who was even more hostile to the foreign religion than Matsunaga and the two judges, protested that exile was too mild a punishment and insisted that Father Vilela and his catechist Lorenzo should die if their doctrine proved contrary to reason. He furthermore suggested they invite Vilela and Lorenzo to Nara, ask them many questions and kill them on the spot if they were found to be guilty.

Takayama's advice was accepted. Yûki, who happened to conduct a civil process for a Christian with the name of Diogo, asked his client many questions about his religion and was struck by his clever answers. Diogo insisted that he knew very little since he had been baptized only recently and that Vilela and Lorenzo could give him more satisfactory answers. Thereupon Yûki dispatched him with a letter to Sakai, where the missionaries had fled on account of the impending danger, and begged the two to come to Nara and instruct him in the Christian religion. From some of the sources it would appear that Yûki was honestly looking for the truth, but in view of what Takayama had suggested one is rather inclined to believe that he wanted to trap the missionaries.

Father Vilela could hardly trust his eyes when he saw Yûki's letter. Was it possible that the man, who heretofore had been known as a bitter enemy and who had agreed to be used as a tool for the destruction of the Church and her ministers, had so completely changed his mind that he should desire to be become a Christian? The priest could not believe it, yet on the other hand he felt inclined to go to Nara no matter what might await him there, for if Yûki was really honest, it would be a pity to miss this wonderful opportunity. However, he thought it wiser to consult his Christians as to what he should do. They were of the opinion that Yûki was not altogether honest and that the priest should by no means expose himself to the danger of being killed, thus leaving them without a pastor. Hence they proposed to send Lorenzo alone to Nara to inquire into Yûki's real intentions. If Lorenzo were not to return within six days this would mean that he had been trapped.

At Nara, Lorenzo had numberless questions put to him by the two judges and Takayama, the latter being the most ardent opponent. Yet when he heard for the first time that God was the Creator of all things and that the human soul was immortal, his heart was struck by the grace of God and was filled with deep joy so that he not only capitulated but declared himself convinced of the truth of the Christian religion. He even prevailed upon the two judges to do likewise. Lorenzo was to return to Sakai to inform Vilela of what had hap-

pened and to tell him to come to Nara to receive
the three into the Church. After the lapse of 40
days Yûki sent for Vilela and was baptized together with Kiyohara and Takayama, who was
baptized Dario. Thus the situation was completely
changed: those who had been appointed to investigate and proscribe the foreign religion had become its staunch adherents, to the great chagrin
of Matsunaga. Yûki did not fail to make him realize the change. When he called on him with
Father Vilela, Matsunaga could not help simulat-
ing at least outward friendship and even listened
to the priest's sermon, although in his heart he was
more hostile to Christianity than ever. When soon
after Vilela was conducted to Kyôto by Yûki and
Kiyohara, the bonzes, not knowing what had happened, believed that the Father came as a pris-
oner to be deported and greatly rejoiced. When
presently Yûki's and Kiyohara's families received
baptism their joy was changed into sorrow and
embarrassment.

Converts from the Samurai Class

Together with Yûki, his eldest son, Saemon-no-
jô, had been baptized. This profligate young man
was completely changed by his new religion and
showed an ardent desire to lead his *samurai* friends
to the faith. Having returned to Iimori Castle,

where he served as a retainer of Miyoshi Chôkei, he urged his friends to send for Lorenzo and listen to his sermons. Eager to break the monotony of their idle camp life and also out of curiosity they gladly consented to Saemon's suggestion, and the latter took Lorenzo to Iimori. When these youngsters beheld Lorenzo's ugly face and clumsy manners they laughed at him, but no sooner had he begun to speak than they were under the spell of his remarkable eloquence and listened with deep interest. The result was that no less than seventy-two asked for baptism. Among the converts there were three leading *samurai*: Sanga Hôki-no-Kami, Ikeda Tango-no-Kami and Miki Handayu, who were to do great things for the Church. Sanga and Ikeda were zealous apostles of their retainers and subjects and Miki's son, Paul Miki, was to be one of the twenty-six proto-martyrs of Japan. Yûki Saemon built a church at the foot of the castle, the first regular church in Gokinai. Sanga, who adopted the Christian name of Sancho, changed a Buddhist chapel on Sanga island into a Christian chapel and later constructed a large church on his island.

Takayama Hida-no-Kami

As we have seen above, Takayama Hida-no-Kami was changed from a rabid enemy into a zealous believer in the Christian religion. Soon

51

after receiving baptism he called Lorenzo to his castle at Sawa, in the province of Yamato, to preach to his family and his retainers. As a result, his wife, his three sons and three daughters as well as a goodly number of *samurai,* 150 persons in all, received baptism. Dario's wife was christened Maria, his eldest son, Justus. He was to be one of the most outstanding Christian lords. His Japanese name was Ukon, and in the Jesuits' annual letters he is known as Justus Ucondono (*dono* or *tono* being the equivalent of lord). Dario rejoiced at this great catch and at once built a church in the precincts of the castle. He himself became the sexten, preacher and support of the new congregation. Lorenzo visited Dario's sisters and brothers-in-law also and converted them. Nor did Dario forget to make his old mother at Takayama a Christian. The old lady with her servants heard Lorenzo's sermons and received baptism. A Buddhist mortuary chapel served as a house of prayer and worship.

Not only his nearest relatives but also his closest friends were advised by Takayama to become Christians, and two of them responded to the call. Ishibashi, lord of Tôchi Castle, with a number of retainers received baptism. They greatly edified the pagans by their exemplary life. Kuroda of Yono Castle, his wife and father likewise were received into the Church with about 120 retainers. Shortly after Kuroda died, his widow was urged by her relatives to give up the faith but her daughter later married Takayama Ukon and she herself died reconciled to the Church at Takatsuki, where she had found refuge after the loss of her fief of Yono. The main fruit of the baptism of Yûki and Kiyohara was the conversion of a number of outstanding *samurai* and the spread of the faith among the warrior class. Although none of the newly established churches, except for a time that of Sanga island, experienced prosperity, the fact that the faith spread among the *samurai* was of the utmost importance for the church of Gokinai, for from their ranks came some of the most outstanding Japanese Christians. The conversion of Takayama Dario alone was to have the most far reaching consequences for the future of the entire Japanese mission. Dario himself was a staunch and zealous adherent of the faith, and his valiant son, Ukon, was to do even greater things for the Church. The Takayamas were never particularly blessed with power or earthly goods, but by their zeal and especially by their heroic example they attracted numberless souls to the Church and among them some of the leading men of the time.

The Catholic Church in Japan

Expulsion from the Capital

In January, 1565, Father Vilela received long-desired help in the person of Father Luis Frois. Together with him came Brother Luis d'Almeida to visit the various churches of Gokinai and report on them to the superior of the mission, Father Cosme de Torres. Brother Almeida was greatly impressed and edified by the zeal and exemplary life of the *samurai* Christians and sent a most interesting report on his inspection tour to his brethren in Europe.

After he left for Kyûshû the church of Gokinai was visited by great trials. The ambitious and powerful Matsunaga Hisahide had been aiming at nothing less than complete control of Gokinai and for this reason had planned to assassinate the *shôgun* Yoshiteru, whom he wanted to replace by a figurehead of his own choice. As long as Miyoshi Chôkei lived he could not hope to carry out his ambitious and treacherous plan, but when Miyoshi died he believed that the time had arrived. Instead of openly attacking Yoshiteru he preferred to trap his victim by a most treacherous strategem using as willing tools his own son and the successor and adopted son of Miyoshi Chôkei. Yoshiteru was assassinated and his relatives and friends massacred. Only Yoshiteru's younger brother, Yoshiaki, escaped by fleeing from the prison where he had been interned.

The general upheaval which followed the assassination of the *shôgun* seemed to the enemies of the Church an excellent opportunity to destroy Christianity as well. At first they attempted to kill the missionaries by hired murderers, but the Christian *samurai* being informed of the impending danger armed themselves to protect the Fathers and the church against any possible attack. Seeing that in this way bloodshed was inevitable, Matsunaga, upon the advice of the bonzes, secured an imperial rescript to the effect that the Fathers were to be expelled and the church building confiscated. This time the enemies had their will, and the Fathers had to go into exile.

They withdrew to Sakai and, although they spared no effort to have the imperial rescript revoked, it was to no avail. Neither the friendly members of the Miyoshi clan nor even the powerful Ôtomo Sôrin were able to do anything for them and for nearly four years they were not readmitted to the capital. Only the mighty word of the powerful warlord, Oda Nobunaga, who was rising at that time, could accomplish in a moment what others had attempted in vain for so many years.

It was due to Takayama Dario's zeal that Nobunaga became a protector and friend of the mission-

aries. Dario was a close friend of Wada Koremasa
who like so many others was advised by him to
become a Christian. He once came with Dario to
the church of Kyôto when the *shôgun* Yoshiteru
was still living. He was deeply impressed by
Lorenzo's sermon and resolved to become a Christian. After his return to his own fief in Kôga, in the
province of Ômi, he asked for a Brother to instruct
him in the faith, but meanwhile the assassination
of Yoshiteru occurred and when the Brother arrived at Kôga, Wada was absent. He was calling
on various lords to obtain their help for Yoshiteru's
younger brother, Yoshiaki, who had fled to Kôga.
Meanwhile war had broken out between the Miyoshi and Matsunaga Hisahide as a result of which
Takayama was ousted from Sawa Castle. Thereupon he joined the army of his friend, Wada Koremasa, who had meanwhile induced the great warlord, Oda Nobunaga, to lend his help to Yoshiaki
and to have him installed *shôgun* in place of his
deceased brother, Yoshiteru.

Within a short time Nobunaga crushed Yoshiaki's enemies and led him in triumph to Kyôto,
where Emperor Ôgimachi installed him as *shôgun*.
Wada Koremasa by his faithful service had won
the good favor of both Nobunaga and Yoshiaki,
and so Takayama Dario resolved to avail himself
of the intercession of his powerful friend, Wada, to

have the missionaries readmitted to the capital.
When Wada approached Nobunaga his request was
granted at once and so he charged Takayama to
bring the missionaries back to the capital. Thus
their exile came to an unexpected end, despite the
opposition of the bonzes and without the formal revocation of the imperial rescript.

Wada was eager to introduce Father Frois, since
Veila had meanwhile been recalled to Kyûshû, to
his powerful lord Nobunaga. On the Father's first
visit Nobunaga declined to meet him, but Wada
arranged for a second visit, and this time Nobunaga
talked familiarly with Father Frois and Lorenzo
on the drawbridge of the *shôgun's* palace. From
then on Nobunaga was a friend of Christianity and
frequently had interviews with the missionaries.
The recall of the Fathers occured in the spring of
1569 when Nobunaga had come to Kyôto for a
visit of about three months. During this time Wada
succeeded in having the church restored to the
Fathers and in obtaining Nobunaga's official permit of residence and many additional favors. The
enemies, nevertheless, did all in their power to
oust them once more from the capital. Their greatest foe was the ex-bonze, Nichijô Shônin, an un-
educated man but a shrewd and dangerous plotter.
He repeatedly urged Nobunaga to expel the Fathers
from the capital but did not succeed. When both

Nichijô and Father Frois happened to be in his presence Nobunaga mischievously provoked a disputation between the two. Frois presented his arguments on the immortality of the soul through his interpreter Lorenzo so powerfully that Nichijô not knowing what to answer seized Nobunaga's sword from the wall and threatened to kill Lorenzo so as to see whether anything of his soul was left in his dead body. Nobunaga and the *daimyô* who were present snatched the sword from Nichijô's hands and the former strongly rebuked him for fighting with arms rather than with arguments. Nichijô, who had lost face, swore fearful revenge but waited until Nobunaga had left for Gifu, where he usually resided.

Having been appointed supervisor of the reconstruction work at the imperial palace by Nobunaga, Nichijô enjoyed the favor of the emperor. He knew very well that Nobunaga had disregarded the imperial rescript when he recalled Father Frois from Sakai and because of this irregularity hoped to expel the missionaries again from the capital. He secured another imperial rescript to the effect that the preachers of the Gospel were to be exiled once more, but he did not dare carry it out without the approval of both the *shôgun* and Nobunaga. The *shôgun* refused, but it was feared that in the long run he would give in, and even Nobunaga seemed to be inclined to sacrifice the Fathers to Nichijô's plotting. The only reliable friend of the missionaries was Wada Koremasa. Realizing the impending danger he sent Frois and Lorenzo to Nobunaga's residence at Gifu and, through the good offices of powerful friends, Nobunaga promised to protect them against Nichijô's machinations. When at last Nichijô incurred Nobunaga's disgrace the danger was definitely averted.

IV

Progress in Kyushu

Almeida's Visit to Satsuma

It will be recalled that Father Gago and his companions were received with extreme kindness by Shimazu Takahisa when, in 1552, they landed in Satsuma. The *daimyô* had changed his former attitude towards Christianity and by a change of policy he hoped to get a share in the lucrative Portuguese trade. Yet it was to be a number of years before these hopes assumed tangible shape. Great therefore was Shimazu's joy when in 1561 a Portuguese junk dropped anchor at Kyôdomari, a small port of Satsuma. When the captain, Mendonça, and a number of his crew decided to go to Bungo to make their confession, Shimazu gave them a letter for Father Torres in which he urgently asked for missionaries.

Thereupon Torres sent Brother Almeida and a

Japanese companion to Satsuma, where they arrived late in December, 1561. Almeida first visited the small congregation of Ichiki which received him with extreme joy and asked many questions about Francis Xavier and about the conditions and the progress of the Church in Bungo, Kyôto and other places. They also told him of miraculous cures worked by the Lord through the relics, especially his own scourge, which Xavier had left with them. He baptized nine adults and a number of babies, two of them children of the lord of the place.

From Ichiki, Brother Almeida went to Kagoshima to visit Shimazu and to thank him for his invitation. The *daimyô* received him with great courtesy and listened attentively to the discourse of his companion on the innumerable benefits of the Lord. On leaving Shimazu the Brother received from him letters for the Viceroy of India, who was urged to send missionaries and ships to Satsuma. From Kagoshima Almeida accompanied Mendonça and his crew to Kyôdomari. Because of the severe winter, the poor food and particularly the unwholesome drinking water nearly all the sailors became sick but Almeida succeeded in curing them. A number of pagans came for instruction and nine of them were baptized. After a stay of two weeks Almeida returned to Kagoshima.

A number of Christians came faithfully to the

sermons but scarcely any pagans were seen among them because they were afraid of the bonzes. Hence Almeida resolved to get in touch with some of the leading Buddhists. Knowing that Xavier had been the friend of the abbot of the Fukushôji Zen monastery, he paid a visit to that place. Old Ninshitsu had died in 1556, but his successor, who likewise had known Xavier, received him most courteously. Having healed him from eye trouble, Brother Almeida became his close friend. The learned bonze asked many questions, which Xavier had been unable to answer because he did not know enough Japanese and had not employed a skilful interpreter. Another bonze, a friend of the former and abbot of the Nanrinji Monastery, likewise called on Almeida and became greatly attached to him. The two bonzes were so much impressed by his discourses that they expressed the desire to be baptized on condition that he would allow them to retain their offices and to practice Zen Buddhism at least outwardly. This Brother Almeida would not and could not concede.

The Brother's friendship with such outstanding personalities encouraged many pagans to listen to his sermons. Thirty-six persons, among them two of the leading men of Shimazu's court, received baptism. A house of prayer was established and served as a temporary church. During the four months which he stayed in Satsuma Almeida at various times visited the Christians of Ichiki, instructed them and administered about seventy baptisms. In the midst of this fruitful activity the Brother was suddenly summoned to Bungo to negotiate with the *daimyô* of Ômura, who greatly desired to see the Christian law spread among his subjects. Thereupon the two bonzes again urged Almeida to baptize them and even promised to give up their positions, but since time did not allow a thorough instruction he promised them that soon a priest would be sent to receive them into the Church. As a matter of fact it was many years before a missionary again appeared in Satsuma.

Ômura Sumitada, the First Christian Daimyô

The hostility of Matsura Takanobu of Hirado and the barrenness of the apostolate in Bungo seemed to endanger the future of the mission in Kyûshû. Hence Father Torres conceived the idea of approaching some other *daimyô,* who might be willing to protect the missionaries and who could offer ports as good as Hirado, which had become the most favored landing place for the Portuguese merchants. Ômura Sumitada, *daimyô* of the small principality of the same name, seemed inclined and able to satisfy Torres' expectations. Brother Almeida was assigned to open negotiations as early as 1561. When the port of Yokoseura was sounded by a Portuguese pilot and found satisfactory, Ômura's governor, Ise-no-Kami, made the following offer: the Father could freely preach in the Ômura district and could directly negotiate with his lord about his conversion to Chrisianity. With this answer Almeida returned to Bungo and was subsequently sent to Satsuma, as we have seen in the preceding section.

During the Brother's absence, a Japanese Christian continued the negotiations with Ômura's governor, and, finally, Sumitada himself made this most generous offer: Yokoseura was to be donated to the Church and should harbor Christians only; if Portuguese ships were to frequent this port, they would be free of all duties and other charges for ten years. Upon this good news Father Torres recalled Brother Almeida from Satsuma to bring the negotiations with Ômura to a happy end. Ise-no-Kami made the reservation that half of Yokoseura was to belong to his lord, but Father Torres nevertheless accepted. This happened at the beginning of July, 1562.

During Lent in 1563, Sumitada paid his first visit to Father Torres at Yokoseura and Father Torres returned his visit. These visits became more and more frequent, Sumitada listening to many a sermon and the Father advising him to become a Christian. After the lapse of several months the *daimyô* was baptized and christened Bartholemew.

Ômura Sumitada was the first *daimyô* to embrace Christian religion, although at about the same time in Gokinai a number of *samurai* of high rank, those whom one might call barons, adopted the Christian religion. Whereas Ômura was undoubtedly moved by the hope of material gain to take this step, Yûki, Kiyohara, Sanga, Ikeda-no-Kami and, above all, Takayama became Christians entirely out of conviction and the desire for salvation.

Consequences of Ômura's Conversion

Ômura Sumitada was the younger brother of Arima Yoshisada, lord of the small principality of Arima, and had been adopted into the Ômura family. His good luck in attracting the Macao ships to his port of Yokoseura by favoring Christianity had convinced his elder brother that it was good policy to do likewise and thus share the lucrative trade. Yoshisada consequently asked for missionaries and suggested they open a mission at Kuchinotsu, the best port of his land.

This mission met with extraordinary success. In spite of temporary difficulties and reverses the entire city very soon embraced the Christian religion. The lord of Shimabara, a vassal and relative of Arima Yoshisada, wanted also a share in the Macao trade and asked for Fathers. In the beginning the mission of Shimabara flourished, but very soon the bonzes stirred up trouble and intimidated the lord to such an extent that he advised the missionaries to leave the country. Thus for a number of years the mission was abandoned and a considerable number of Christians emigrated.

Although at the outset material considerations prompted Ômura to embrace Christianity, he would nevertheless have secured the lion's share in the Macao trade, as a result of the extraordinary privileges he had granted the Fathers and the Portuguese, even if he had not become a Christian. As a matter of fact, Ômura became a Christian out of conviction and remained a staunch member of the Church for the rest of his life. He even showed an excessive and almost fanatic zeal in fighting paganism, particularly by destroying temples and burning images. As a result a dangerous rebellion broke out which aimed at nothing less than his death and the substitution of the bastard son of his adoptive father as successor. Simultaneously Father Torres was to die. The original plan of the rebels was frustrated, and they burned the castle and city of Ômura, but Sumitada managed to escape to a nearby castle and to hold the place against great odds until help was sent by his father, Arima

Haruzumi. Meanwhile the city and church of Yokoseura were burned by the rebels, but the missionaries fled to a Portuguese ship.

Although the rebellion was crushed, for two years no missionary was able to reside in the district of Ômura. From 1565 on, progress was again made. The city and harbor of Yokoseura were not restored and for a short time the port of Fukuda was frequented by the Portuguese instead, but very soon Nagasaki, or Fukae as it was then called, became the principal harbor for the Macao trade. In 1568 Father Vilela started a mission at Nagasaki, converted some 1,500 and changed a temple into a church which he called All Saints Church. In 1571 the first Macao ship dropped anchor at the new port and by 1579 it had become the best and most favored harbor of Kyûshû.

Resumption of the Hirado Mission

Since the expulsion of Father Vilela in 1558 the Jesuits spared no effort to restore the mission of Hirado because it seemed essential for the preservation of the flourishing church on Dom Antonio's islands. There the work of evangelization had not only continued but made considerable progress. It was, nevertheless, not until 1564 that the church of Hirado could be rebuilt with the permission of the *daimyô*, Matsuura Takanobu. Fearing that the

Macao trade might be altogether diverted to Ômura, Takanobu finally gave in and allowed the resumption of the mission and the rebuilding of the church.

Without the staunch support of the fearless Dom Antonio, the Jesuits would never have succeeded in maintaining the mission of Hirado. Whenever the Christians were molested he protested and vigorously demanded satisfaction. A bonze wanted to buy a plot of land from Antonio and when he refused to sell it, the bonze set fire to his estate. Antonio demanded that Matsura punish the culprit and the bonze was exiled. Some ruffians insulted a picture of the Blessed Virgin Mary, and Dom Antonio strongly demanded satisfaction. At another time a large cross had been removed from the Christian cemetery; and Dom Antonio threatened to use violence if no satisfaction was to be given. On the next morning the cross was back in its place.

As long as Dom Antonio lived, the Christians were never again molested by Matsuura Takanobu. Peaceful relations between him and Ômura Sumitada were even restored. Sumitada's daughter, Micia, was given in marriage to Takanobu's grandson, Hisanobu, so that the cordial relations between the two houses might thereby be more firmly established. Before Dom Antonio's death in 1581 his islands of Ikitsuki, Takushima, Ira, Katûga and

The Catholic Church in Japan

Shishi had become entirely Christian.

Death of Silva and Fernandez

In 1564 Brother Duarte da Silva died at Takase, in the province of Higo, the first Jesuit missionary to die in Japan. He was an industrious, humble and pious man. Brother Almeida in his obituary gives high praise to this truly apostolic fellow worker. He extolls his humility, patience and indefatigable zeal. Although of delicate health, he practised severe penance, preached to the neophytes and catechumens and still found time not only to study Japanese but Chinese as well. He composed a Japanese grammar and excellent dictionaries.

Three years later Xavier's faithful companion, Brother Fernandez, died at Hirado. Although a simple and humble lay-brother he had accomplished more than many priests of his Order. Xavier once told one of his foremost disciples, Father Barzaeus, that he was still very far from Fernandez' degree of perfection. Father Torres once said that although Xavier had founded the Church of Japan it would soon have perished without the labors and the zeal of Brother Fernandez. He was, above all, remarkable for his command of Japanese, composed an excellent grammar, translated learned works as well as the Gospels of all Sundays of the year into Japanese, wrote sermons for their explanation and commentaries on the Our Father, the Hail Mary, the Apostles' Creed, the Decalogue and translated many useful and indispensible prayers and treatises. The Christians of Hirado mourned his death and deeply regretted their loss.

New Missions

In 1563 the lord of the Gotô Islands asked Father Torres for a doctor. Torres granted his request and together with the doctor sent a Christian, Diogo, to the islands. The *daimyô* was cured of his illness and asked Diogo to preach. When the latter returned home the *daimyô* begged Father Torres to send missionaries to his land. It was only after three years that Father Torres could comply with his request and send Brothers Almeida and Lorenzo to the islands. They arrived in January, 1566. They were kindly received and began preaching, but when the *daimyô* suddenly fell ill, it was attributed to the presence of the missionaries. Thus the sermons were boycotted. Although Brother Almeida cured the lord of his sickness, he nevertheless, remained indifferent and unresponsive towards the Christian religion. Thereupon the Brother asked Father Torres to recall him to Bungo. Many relatives of the *daimyô* and a good number of other people were healed by Brother Almeida, but he would not accept any financial reward for

71

his charitable help. He eventually conquered the heart of the lord, who greatly urged him to remain. He consented, and the preaching of the Gospel was resumed. The *daimyô* himself as well as fifty *samurai* came regularly to the sermons, and twenty-five persons asked for and received baptism. In two other places Brother Almeida established small congregations, but because of illness he had to leave. Lorenzo alone remained in the islands.

Towards the end of 1566 Father Montes went as the first priest to the new mission but made little headway. A bastard son of the *daimyô* wanted to become a Christian, but the bonzes stirred up trouble and would not allow it. From the fall of 1568 until the beginning of 1570, Father Vallareggio took charge of the Gotô mission. He succeeded in leading the son of the *daimyô* to the faith. In the Jesuit letters he is called Dom Luis. At once the bonzes together with Dom Luis' uncle urged the neophyte to give up his faith and even threatened to kill him, but he remained firm. A good many of Dom Luis' retainers likewise received baptism. At the beginning of 1570 Father Vallareggio had to leave Japan because of ill health and subsequently the mission was visited only occasionally by a priest or a brother.

In the summer of 1566 a mission was started at Shiki on the northwest coast of Shimojima, one of the two great islands of the Amakusa Archipelago, west of Kyûshû. The lord of the land had adopted a son of the *daimyô* of Arima and was eager, like Ômura and his elder brother, Arima Yoshisada, to have a share in the Macao trade. Because of this he asked for missionaries, but for several years his request could not be granted because of the scarcity of workers. At last Brother Almeida after his return from Gotô was put in charge of the new mission. The Brother urged the prince to receive baptism but at first he refused on the plea that it might lead to rebellion like Ômura's. Very soon a Portuguese ship arrived and the prince urged Brother Almeida to baptize him. The Brother hesitated for a while, but when he was assured by the principal retainers that their lord was absolutely honest, he received him into the Church together with 500 others. Very soon, however, his neophyte built an Amida temple and urged the Christians to give up the faith. This they would not do and not a few preferred to emigrate to Nagasaki. The apostate prince thereupon sent his emissaries to that city to kill two of the leading emigrants. In spite of these trials the mission of Shiki was not given up, for the apostate prince did not expel the missionaries and even tolerated the conversion of his people. The number of Christians increased from year to year until by

1571 it had reached the imposing figure of 2,000.

About the time Brother Almeida began to work at Shiki the lord of Kawachinoura (near Hondo, the present capital of the Amakusa Archipelago), Amakusa Izu-no-Kami, asked for missionaries. He was prompted, like so many others, by the desire to share the benefits of the Macao trade. Only after the lapse of three years was Torres able to comply with his request. Again it was Brother Almeida who was entrusted with the foundation of the new mission because of his extraordinary talent in overcoming initial difficulties by skilful negotiation. Cautioned by the experience at Shiki he was on guard not to be duped by another prince mainly interested in commercial gain. Having stayed for about twenty days, he feigned departure. Thereupon Amakusa grew very sad and urged him to remain, but Almeida would agree only on condition. Permission was to be granted to preach and to administer baptism to all who were to ask for it; Amakusa himself was to listen to the sermons for eight days; after the lapse of these eight days one of his sons was to receive baptism; a piece of land for building a church was to be donated and Amakusa was to give special assurance that all people living between Kawachinoura and Shiki should enjoy complete freedom of conscience. Amakusa accepted these conditions and Almeida began to work.

For ten days Amakusa, with many retainers, listened to the sermons. His governor, who was christened Leo, with fifty of his people, received baptism. In the rest of the fief 400 others were received into the Church. In view of such striking success the bonzes became alarmed and allied themselves with Amakusa's brothers, demanding that Leo be killed. To this Amakusa would not consent and instead begged Leo to to leave the country for a time. In his heart Amakusa was always friendly to the Christian religion, and if under pressure he sacrificed Leo and even had to advise Almeida to withdraw for a time, he always remained a friend and protector of the Church and was, moreover, encouraged by Ôtomo Sôrin to favor the Christians and the missionaries. Even when his brothers openly rebelled and almost conquered his fief, he remained true to his pro-Christian policy. When the rebellion had been crushed he received baptism and remained a fervent Christian until his death.

State of the Japanese Mission at the End of 1570

Father Vilela because of ill health was compelled to leave for India in 1570. From Goa, October 20, 1571, he wrote a letter in which he gives an interesting report on the Japanese mission. He writes that when he arrived in Japan in July, 1556, there were no more than 500 Christians and only two churches in the Jesuit mission, whereas now there were about 30,000 Christians and 40 churches. It must be noted, however, that he greatly underestimates the number of Christians at the time of his arrival, for they numbered at least 4,000 (2,000 in Bungo, 500 Hirado, 1,500 to 2,000 at Yamaguchi and several hundreds at Kagoshima). Even so the increase during the 14 years of his stay in Japan was truly remarkable.

These are Father Vilela's statistics: Hirado 5,000, Ômura 2,500, Nagasaki 1,500, Fukuda 1,200, Kabashima 400, Gotô 2,000, Shiki 2,000, Amakusa (Kawachinoura) 40, Kuchinotsu 3,000 (i.e. the entire population), Shimabara 800, Satsuma 300, Bungo 5,000, Yamaguchi 1,000, Kyôto and neighborhood 1,500. The figures for Bungo are most certainly exaggerated, for until Ôtomo's conversion in 1578 there were never more than 2,500 Christians in that province. If the figure for Yamaguchi has been decreased considerably this is easily explained by the dispersion of a great many Christians, especially Christian *samurai*. Thus the seed planted by St. Francis Xavier had borne rich fruit, and in the following seventeen years the number of Christians increased even more.

V

Rapid Growth

Preliminary Remarks

With the year 1570 missionary work in Japan entered a new phase. Until then there had been progress in spite of numerous reverses. In Kyûshû, Ômura Sumitada had embraced the Christian religion; his brother, Arima Yoshisada, had called the Fathers to his principal port of Kuchinotsu; new centers had been established in the Gotô and Amakusa Archipelagos; and Ôtomo Sôrin was still a protector and friend of the missionaries as he had been since he had met Saint Francis Xavier. Yet there had been great reverses also, particularly at Yamaguchi and Hirado, and the fruits of Ômura's conversion could not be gathered because of the fierce rebellions with which the neo-converts were faced time and again. In Bungo the work of evangelization did not make much progress, since Christianity was believed to be the religion of the poor and the sick and, above all, because Ôtomo himself could not make up his mind to become a Christian. In Gokinai, Nobunaga greatly favored the Church, but the number of Christians was still very small.

In 1570 Father Francisco Cabral, S.J., was sent from India to visit the mission and to replace Father Torres as superior. Torres had done very good work, but he himself more than anyone else realized that he was too old to direct a mission which called for a man of robust health and strong will to overcome the difficulties piling up on all sides. He therefore was only too glad to hand over the direction to a younger and stronger man such as Father Cabral undoubtedly was. Before the year drew to an end Father Torres was dead.

Father Cabral, of noble Portuguese stock, had been a soldier in India before he joined the Society of Jesus. Although his ambitious ideals had thereby undergone a radical change, he, nevertheless, retained until his death the enthusiasm and vigorous energy of his former career. Even before his ordination he had been master of novices; eight years after his entrance into the Order he became rector of the college of Bassein and from then until 1597 he held one important position after another. He was a man of strong will, a real leader, who knew how to inspire those under his direction with his own enthusiasm.

Japan needed just such a man. The vigorous growth of the mission during the years of Cabral's superiorate testifies to his ability as a leader. He was of the opinion that the princes were the best helpers of the missionaries, since their will was law to their subjects, and so he spared no effort to draw as many of them as possible to the Church. The conversion of Amakusa, Arima Yoshisada and, above all, that of Ôtomo Sôrin was to no small extent the fruit of his tireless zeal. Even if he was unable to convert Nobunaga, he was, nevertheless, greatly honored by the mighty warlord. This again had far reaching effects in Kyûshû.

From this it does not follow, however, that Father Cabral was an ideal superior in every respect, as will be seen later.

Progress in Central Japan

The number of Christians in the capital of Kyôto had always been small and increased very little from 1570 to 1579. It was, nevertheless, considered indispensible for the prestige of the mission to have a splendid church in the capital where all of the principal Buddhist sects had their luxurious temples. The plans for the new church were drawn up by Father Organtino in European style, but the interior was to be strictly according to

The Catholic Church in Japan

Japanese taste. Since the building ground was very small and none of the hostile neighbors was willing to sell additional land to the Fathers, they were compelled to erect a three-floor structure. Thereupon violent opposition arose on the part of the bonzes, who considered it an insult that the Christian church should stand out over their one-floor temples. In spite of all opposition the Fathers had their will, since the governor of the city and Nobunaga both favored them.

On August 15, 1577, the new church was dedicated in honor of the Assumption of Our Lady. The Christians of the city and the Christian lords of Gokinai had generously contributed to the great work so that the new structure aroused the admiration of all, even the enemies. The fact that this church looms so large in the anti-Christian novels of the later Tokugawa period where it is called *Nanbanji* ("temple of the Southern barbarians") is a tangible proof that it must have greatly impressed its contemporaries.

Christian Leaders in Central Japan

The bulk of the Christians in Central Japan lived not in the capital but in the various fortresses, the commanders of which were staunch Christians. The most powerful of them was Naitô Tadatoshi, lord of Kameyama in the Province of Tanba. From a Christian lady who had fled from Yamaguchi to Tanba he had received his first knowledge of Christianity. He then went to Kyôto to learn more about it, listened to the sermons and was baptized by Father Luis Frois, probably about 1570. His example was followed by many of his retainers, for, when in 1573 he came to Kyôto with 2,000 *samurai* to help *shôgun* Yoshiaki in his struggle with Nobunaga, their Christian banners aroused general admiration. Unfortunately Yoshiaki was defeated and driven from the capital, and Naitô was stripped of his fief and followed his suzerain into exile. His Christian retainers probably accompanied him, for henceforth there is never again mention of a Christian congregation at Kameyama.

Joam Yûki, commander of Okayama Castle and a relative of Yûki Yamashiro-no-Kami, founded a Christian community of *samurai* in that city. He was aided by his zealous uncle, Yûki Yaheiji. It would seem, however, that not many of the common people became Christians, for when Yûki went from Okayama to Sangajima, the fine church at Okayama became deserted and was eventually transferred to Ôsaka. Evidently most of the Christians were *samurai* who moved with their lord to the new fief, as was the general custom in those days. When Joam Yûki lost his life in the battle

The Catholic Church in Japan

of Komakiyama, Yaheiji took service with the
Christian admiral, Konishi Yukinaga, first on the
island of Shôdoshima, later in Konishi's new fief in
southern Higo. After Konishi's death in 1600 he
became a retainer of Katô Kiyomasa but was soon
compelled to seek refuge in Arima because he refused to give up his faith. When the Christian lord
of Arima turned away from the Church in 1612
Yaheiji had once more to go into exile for the sake
of Christ.

Among the earliest and most zealous Christian
lords in Gokinai were Sancho Sanga and his son,
Mancio. They were from Sangajima, a group of
tiny islands in a lake—today only rice fields—
at the foot of Iimori Castle in the province of Kawachi. During the years of exile, 1565 to 1569,
the beautiful church of Sangajima was the rallying
point of the Christians of the capital and its surroundings. Very soon all inhabitants of Sangajima,
about 4,000 or 5,000 souls, adopted the Christian
religion. Unfortunately in 1582 the Sanga took
sides with the traitor, Akechi Mitsuhide, who had
destroyed Nobunaga. After Mitsuhide's defeat a
punitive expedition was launched against Sangajima, and the beautiful church was burned. Only
by a timely flight did the Sangas escape death.
Although they clung to their Christian faith, they
never again rose to prominence. Sangajima was

given to the Christian Yûki but when Joam Yûki was killed in battle Sangajima received a pagan lord. On the further fate of this once florishing church we have no information whatever.

Together with Sancho Sanga and Miki Handayu, Simeon Ikeda Tango-no Kami had been baptized at Iimori Castle in 1563. He also proved a staunch Christian and led many of his retainers of Yao and Wakae Castles to the faith. After Hideyoshi's rise to power he was transferred to another place where his Christian *samurai* followed him. Apparently there were no Christians left at either Yao or Wakae.

Among the *samurai* churches of Gokinai only the one at Takatsuki Castle was of any importance. We have seen how Takayama Hida-no-Kami after having been a bitter enemy of Christianity was converted by Brother Lorenzo at Nara. At that time he was lord of Sawa Castle and a vassal of Matsunaga Hisahide. After Matsunaga's defeat he was ousted from Sawa Castle and took service with his friend Wada Koremasa, lord of Takatsuki Castle. In 1573, two years after Wada Koremasa's death, Takatsuki Castle passed to the Takayama as a subfief of Araki Murashige, lord of the province of Settsu.

Takatsuki was a fief with a yearly income of 20,000 *ducats* and the entire population was still pagan when the Takayamas took possession of their new domain. What the Takayamas were lacking in wealth and power was more than made up by their marvellous zeal for the spread of the Gospel. When Father Cabral visited the place in 1574 some 120 *samurai* were instructed and baptized. In 1576 no less than 4,000 baptisms were administered, and in 1579 there were 8,000 Christians at Takatsuki.

During the following years the fief was twice enlarged in size and doubled in revenue and population. When, in 1585, the Takayamas were changed to Akashi all 30,000 inhabitants of Takatsuki had become Christians. This marvellous growth was due, in the main, to the truly apostolic zeal of the heroic figure Takayama Ukon, one of the greatest men of the time.

Mass Conversions in Kyûshû

The years between 1570 and 1578 were marked by a mass movement towards the Church inaugurated by the conversion of a number of ruling princes. These conversions were motivated, to a great extent, by the hope of sharing the lucrative Macao trade, whereas in Gokinai it was solely the persuasive power of Christian truth and personal conviction which drew men like Sanga, Yûki Ikeda and Takayama Dario to the Christian faith. Even

84

if the first incentive to conversion for the majority
of the Kyûshû lords was the hope for temporal gain,
they nevertheless embraced the new faith with
great enthusiasm and firm conviction. They, moreover, spared no effort to win over their subjects to
their new faith with the result that very soon great
mass conversions occurred. We need not approve
of all their methods, particularly moral pressure
and even physical force, but the fact remains that
in this way compact Christian communities arose,
which in part have kept their faith until the present day, despite the most awful and systematic of
persecutions.

As we have seen Ômura Sumitada was baptized
as early as 1563, but as a result of his reckless and
fanatic zeal he was faced with a most dangerous
rebellion. Although he eventually mastered the
situation, the work of evangelization for many
years made but slight progress. According to
Vilela's statistics there were in the entire fief of
Ômura no more than 5,600 Christians in 1571. In
1574, Sumitada was threatened by another rebellion
led by his brother-in-law, lord of Isahaya, who
wanted to kill him and obtain his fief. He was
allied with the lords of Hirado and Gotô and even
had a secret understanding with Ômura's brother,
Yoshisada of Arima. The bonzes of Ômura and the
majority of Sumitada's *samurai* were entangled in

the rebellion. In spite of the desperate situation Sumitada almost miraculously triumphed over his enemies and his unfaithful retainers returned to their duty once they realized that he was going to win.

Having crushed the rebellion Ṣumitada resolved to stamp out paganism. The bonzes were urged to listen to the sermons of the Fathers. Those who chose to be baptized were allowed to marry and to retain their income, but those who would not become Christians were compelled to leave the country. Out of 100 bonzes only two preferred exile to baptism. During the year 1575 more than 20,000 pagans were baptized and an almost equal number in the following year. In 1577 not a single pagan was left in Sumitada's fief. The Christians numbered from 50,000 to 60,000 souls.

The mission of Amakusa-Kawachinoura had just been started when Father Vilela published his statistics of the Japanese mission in 1571. Hence there were only about 40 Christians in this newly established center. In spite of the treacherous intentions of his nearest relatives, the lord of the place, Amakusa Izu-no-Kami, protected the missionaries, although he asked them to withdraw for a time. When he had finally crushed the rebellion the number of Christians increased rapidly and the prince himself asked for baptism. He adopted the

Christian name of Michael. One of the most stubborn enemies of Christianity was Michael's wife, but when, in 1577, she also received baptism and took the name Donna Gracia, she became the most zealous protagonist of Christianity so that in 1579 the entire fief, about 10,000 souls, was Christian.

Even before Ômura Sumitada's baptism his elder brother, Arima Yoshisada, lord of Arima, had invited the missionaries to his principal port of Kuchinotsu. After the lapse of a few years the entire city had become Christian. Although Sumitada did all in his power to win over his elder brother to his new religion, the various rebellions in Ômura evidently warned Yoshisada not to follow Sumitada's advice. He was also perhaps somewhat jealous of his younger brother's monopolization of the Macao trade.

It was probably for this reason that he was entangled in the rebellion of 1574. The lord of Isahaya had told him that he wanted to assassinate Sumitada on his way to Obama, where the two brothers were to meet. Yoshisada thereupon warned his brother of the imminent danger and simultaneously urged him to give up his faith, save his life and preserve his fief. Sumitada refused and Yoshisada did not attempt to stop the lord of Isahaya from carrying out his wicked plan. He was thus at least indirectly involved in the fratricidal plot.

The Catholic Church in Japan

Sumitada happily escaped the threatening danger and, moreover, gained a victory over all his enemies. Emboldened by this success he began to stamp out paganism in his land and met with no resistance whatever. Yoshisada was greatly impressed, lost all fear of possible rebellion and considered becoming a Christian himself. The conversion of Ôtomo Sôrin's second son cleared away the last apprehensions and he asked for baptism. He was baptized by Father Gaspar Coelho in 1576 and christened Andrew. Simultaneously a great many of his *samurai* were received into the Church so that the total number of Christians in Arima rose to the impressive figure of 15,000.

Yoshisada was accidentally hurt the following year and died soon afterwards. This sudden death was interpreted by the bonzes as a just punishment by the gods of the country, and they urged Yoshisada's youthful son and successor, Harunobu, to stamp out Christianity. The weak youngster let them have their will, with the result that the crosses were cut down and the church of Arima destroyed. The Christians were urged to return to paganism, and since many of them had embraced the faith only recently and without sufficient instruction or firm conviction, a great many grew weak. Others, particularly the entire city of Kuchinotsu, remained so firm that Harunobu began to despair of victory and abstained from further molestations. Thereupon many of the apostates asked for readmission to the Church.

Up to the end of 1575 the Church made very little progress in Bungo. The few Christians there were almost entirely from the lowest ranks of society and most of them had been prompted to receive baptism by the charitable help they had received from the Fathers. Only one nobleman had embraced the Christian religion, and he had done so while he was under medical treatment in the mission hospital. Having recovered his health he was ashamed of his faith.

The desperate situation of the Bungo mission underwent a sudden and radical change for the better by the conversion of several of Ôtomo Sôrin's nearest relatives, particularly his second son, Chikaie. According to the general custom of the time, the younger sons of ruling princes were made abbots of famous and rich temples to prevent their plotting against their elder brothers. Ôtomo Sôrin had built a magnificent temple with a large revenue for his second son, but Chikaie refused most stubbornly to become a bonze. His father was greatly embarrassed at his refusal, and since Chikaie was a very unruly and obstinate youngster, he suggested that he might become a Christian and thus learn to check his unbridled passions. The boy gladly consented and after due instruction was baptized under the Christian name of Sebastian. This happened shortly before Christmas, 1575.

The result of this conversion was a complete change in the attitude of the nobility towards the Christian religion. Many of the highest rank asked for baptism, and since Sebastian refused to admit anyone to his intimate companionship who was not a Christian, many young *samurai* became Christians and by their reformed life proved themselves sincere.

Even a little before Sebastian's conversion, Ôtomo Sôrin's son-in-law, Ichijô Kanesada, had been baptized and adopted the Christian name of Paul. He had fled to Bungo, having been ousted from his fief of Tosa in Shikoku by his rebellious vassal, Chôsokabe Motochika. Hoping to recover his land and to lead it to the Christian faith, he returned to Tosa. He suffered defeat from Chôsokabe and was reduced to one fortress near the coast. He, nevertheless, remained a convinced Christian until his death.

Not long after Sebastian's baptism, Tawara Chikatora, adopted son of Ôtomo's brother-in-law, Tawara Chikakata, asked to be admitted into the Church. Once his adopted father had taken him to the church the boy became so attached to the Fathers that he asked to be instructed in the Christian religion. When he witnessed a miracle in the church (a devil had been cast out) he was so deeply impressed that he asked for baptism. Thereupon there arose violent opposition.

Ôtomo's wife, whom on account of her hatred of Christianity the Fathers called Jezebel, together with her brother, Chikatora's adopted father, Chika-kata, spared no effort to prevent the boy's baptism. They tried his constancy first with promises and, as he remained firm, they threatened to disinherit him and send him back to his parents in Kyôto. Chikakata even attempted to enlist the support of Father Cabral by promising to favor Christianity if the Father should prevail upon his son to re-main a pagan. To this Cabral could of course not agree and so Jezebel and Chikakata resolved to kill the Fathers and stamp out Christianity. Elaborate preparations were made for the assassination of both Fathers and Christians, and the plot was to be carried out while Ôtomo and his eldest son, Yoshimune, were out of town.

The Fathers, informed of the impending danger, hurriedly sent word to Ôtomo of what was happen-ing, and were assured of his help. Ôtomo hurried back and gave strict orders for the protection of the Christians. He permitted Chikatora to receive baptism and promised to favor him if his father were to reject or disinherit him for becoming a

Christian. Seeing that Jezebel was the ultimate instigator of all the trouble, he resolved to repudiate her and marry another lady, who was to be a Christian.

Despite Jezebel's and Chikakata's protests and lamentations Ôtomo dismissed his wife and married the mother-in-law of his second son, Sebastian. Next he asked the Fathers to instruct his new wife and receive her into the Church. She was baptized under the Christian name of Julia. The Fathers had been hoping for more than 26 years for Ôtomo's conversion, and the numberless favors he had bestowed upon them assured them that some day the Lord would reward his generosity by leading him to the faith. Their hope was not frustrated, for while his new wife was being instructed Ôtomo himself attended public instructions and asked for a Brother to teach him the Christian doctrine. At last he was baptized on August 28, 1578, and in grateful memory of his saintly friend, Xavier, he adopted his Christian name of Francisco.

Ôtomo's conversion made a deep impression upon his contemporaries, for he was considered one of the wisest men in the country and one of the most powerful princes of the empire. His step could not be called rash or void of sober reasoning, for he had waited twenty-seven years before he took it. Nor was he prompted by the hope for commercial gain, since long ago the Macao ships had ceased to visit his ports. His conversion encouraged and confirmed the Christian *daimyô* in Kyûshû in their faith and prepared the way for the conversion of others, particularly Arima Harunobu, who had tried in vain to destroy Christianity in his domain. But the most tangible results of Ôtomo's conversion were witnessed in Bungo itself. Up to the year 1578 there were no more than 2,500 Christians, but before another year elapsed the number rose to 6,000.

Two Crises

Shortly after his conversion Ôtomo Sôrin resolved to reconquer the large province of Hyûga from Shimazu Yoshihisa of Satsuma, who had ousted the Itôs from their domain and compelled them to seek refuge with their powerful relatives in Bungo. Even before receiving baptism Sôrin had abdicated in favor of his eldest son, Yoshimune, who therefore accompanied his father with a powerful army to Hyûga. In the beginning all went well but, because of Yoshimune's and Tawara Chikakata's incapability, the Bungo army was defeated so completely that Sôrin could scarcely save himself by a precipitate flight to Bungo. Until then he had always been successful in his many wars, but from then on the house of Ôtomo suffered defeat after defeat because Yoshimune proved utterly incapable of holding together what he had inherited from his great father. In the various provinces which in former years Sôrin had conquered, native barons rebelled and joined hands with the enemy, and even in Bungo itself mighty vassals plotted against their legitimate suzerain.

The enemies of the Church, even those who stood loyally by their lord, clamorously declared the plight of the Ôtomos to be a punishment of the enraged national deities, both *Shintô* and Buddhist, whom Sôrin had abandoned and Yoshimune was about to give up. They urged the cowardly Yoshimune to return to the religion of his ancestors and to expel the missionaries, and Yoshimune was weak enough to yield to their threats. Sôrin, learning of it, declared that as long as he lived he would not permit the Christians or missionaries to suffer any harm, even if he had to die with them. This courageous language did not fail to impress his loyal vassals and they begged him to lead them against the rebels and restore order. Sôrin's courage and constancy had saved the situation and averted disaster. Misfortune had not shaken his faith.

While Bungo was in turmoil the church of Gokinai was faced with an equally dangerous crisis. Nobunaga, the protector of the Christians, was threatened by a powerful league. The mighty Môri, who ruled all the western provinces of Honshû, had formed an alliance with Kôsa Kennyo, head of the warlike Honganji Buddhist sect. Araki Murashige, to whom Nobunaga had given the province of Settsu, had treacherously joined Nobunaga's foes. If Nobunaga were to succumb in the forthcoming struggle, the Church was doomed, for Kôsa and the Môri hated Christianity, and what made the situation even more desperate was the fact that the Takayamas, the pillars of the Church in Gokinai, were Araki's vassals and could not remain neutral in the impending war. If they stood by their suzerain Araki, they would draw Nobunaga's revenge upon the Church; if on the other hand they were to join Nobunaga, they would incur the reproach of treason and expose themselves and all Christians to the revenge of Araki and his allies were they to win the war.

Takayama Ukon, realizing the gravity of the situation, had done everything in his power to separate his suzerain from his allies on the plea that it was immoral to rebel against one's lord and benefactor. He, moreover, pointed out that it was a hopeless proposition to make war on a military genius like Nobunaga. Ukon's reasoning did not fail to impress Araki, and he set out to apologize to Nobunaga for what had happened already and expected to receive his pardon. Things had gone so far now, however, that the war party threatened to depose Araki, if he were to make peace with Nobunaga. Araki was not generous enough to risk his fief or his life in the face of such threats, and so he openly declared war on Nobunaga.

Takayama Ukon was convinced that he could not take part in what appeared to him an unjust war. On the other hand the Japanese code of chivalry demanded from a vassal absolute fidelity to his suzerain, whether he waged a just or an unjust war. If then Ukon were to refuse service to Araki in the impending war, he would be called an unfaithful vassal by his pagan contemporaries. It would mean, moreover, certain death to his younger sister and his only son, whom he had given to Araki as hostages. Father Organtino at once called on Ukon and told him that in good conscience he could not stand by the traitor, Araki. Ukon saw the logic of the Father's reasoning but the terrible fate of his hostages so frightened him that he could not make up his mind to break with Araki.

Meanwhile Nobunaga had appeared with a powerful army at the gates of Takatsuki Castle to take it by storm, for it was the key fortress of Settsu. Viewing the fortress from all sides Nobunaga realized that he could not take it in a quick assault, for Ukon had made it an impregnable bulwark against which even the military genius of Nobunaga was useless. Since, however, Takatsuki was essential in dealing a decisive blow to Araki, Nobunaga resolved to take it through diplomacy of which he was no less a master than of strategy. He summoned Father Organtino to his camp and told him that as a Christian Takayama could not lawfully help the traitor, Araki. Hence the Father was to go to Takatsuki and urge Ukon to hand over the fortress immediately. Thereupon Takayama again tried to separate Araki from his allies and Araki was ready to make peace if Nobunaga would guarantee him his fief. This Nobunaga was unwilling to do, and so the negotiations broke down. Nobunaga interned all the missionaries and sent Father Organtino once more to Takatsuki with the ultimatum that, if Ukon did not immediately hand over the fortress, all missionaries and Christians would be crucified and all churches destroyed.

Ukon suffered agonies, but in the end his Christian conscience gained the victory. He would not hand over Takatsuki to Nobunaga; he would return it; he himself would abdicate as commander, shave his head and present himself unarmed and in a pilgrim's garb in Nobunaga's camp. If he should be killed with the Fathers, he would die a martyr, but if Nobunaga were to spare his life, he would devote the rest of his days to the service of the Church. Explaining everything to his father in a letter he slipped out of Takatsuki and proceeded to Nobunaga's camp. Nobunaga received him with open arms and did not allow him to become a missionary but engaged him to serve as a direct vassal.

When Ukon's father learned what had happened, he was furious and gave strict orders for the defense of the castle, but his Christian *samurai* did not obey him and even shut him from the bastions. Thereupon Dario fled to Araki's camp to save the lives of the hostages. Araki was fair enough to see that Dario had acted as a faithful vassal and that even Ukon had done nothing that would warrant the destruction of innocent hostages. Dario, however, was interned in Arioka Castle. Meanwhile Takatsuki had capitulated and was restored to Ukon with a materially increased revenue.

In the following year Araki was completely routed, but in order to save his life he left his hostages to their fate. Thus Dario was at Nobunaga's mercy and was condemned to death, but considering Ukon's merits, the death sentence was changed to life exile in Echizen. In this way he became the apostle of that province. The crisis had happily passed without baneful effects on the Church. On the contrary, Nobunaga, feeling obliged to the Fathers, even doubled his favors.

VI

Alessandro Valignano, the Visitor

Great Sucess in Arima

On July 25, 1579, the Jesuit Visitor, Alessandro Valignano, landed at Kuchinotsu, the principal port of Arima. It was no mere chance that the Macao ship anchored at Kuchinotsu, for Father Valignano, knowing that Arima Harunobu had not succeeded in his attempt to stamp out Christianity, that he was rather sorry for having persecuted the Church, and that he greatly desired a share in the Macao trade, had advised the Portuguese captain to land in one of Arima's ports.

In this way he hoped to please the young prince and possibly lead him and his country to the faith. He had judged correctly for Harunobu was greatly pleased, visited the Father and apologized for having harassed the Christians. He distinctly gave him to understand that he himself was willing to become a Christian.

Valignano returned Harunobu's visit, but showed no particular hurry to receive him into the Church, since he feared that the changeable young man might easily turn away again if his hopes for temporal gain and material help were not fulfilled to his satisfaction. Hence the Visitor made him wait and demanded guarantees, particularly the conversion of his nearest relatives and principal retainers.

Arima was hard pressed by his powerful enemy, Ryûzôji Takanobu, with whom not a few of his own barons were hand-in-glove. He hoped that by his conversion he would secure the help of his Christian uncle, Ômura Sumitada, and even obtain food and ammunition from the Visitor himself. He accepted all of Valignano's conditions. It was nevertheless seven months before the Father yielded to his importunate pleadings. He was baptized in March, 1580, and adopted the Christian name of Protasius. Simultaneously 4,000 of his *samurai* received baptism and 7,000 Christians who had formerly apostatized were reconciled to the Church. Moreover, temples were destroyed and bonzes were advised to become Christians or leave the country.

Thus the Christianization of the entire fief was expected within a short time, the more so because Ryûzôji had granted an honorable peace and the rebellious barons had been destroyed or brought to submission.

Reorientation of Missionary Methods

When Father Valignano came to Japan he knew nothing about the mission except what he had read in the rosy accounts sent to Europe. Upon his arrival he was confronted with an altogether different situation. The number of Christians had greatly increased within the preceding years, but a great deal of what had been accomplished was subsequently destroyed by revolutions and apostacies.

The Fathers had been expelled from Yamaguchi more than 23 years before. In Hirado the ruling prince had urged the Christians to apostatize; in Gotô the apostacy of the prince, Don Luis, had led nearly all Christians astray, in Arima the majority of the 12,000 Christians had grown weak when Harunobu persecuted the Church, and the defeat of the Ôtomos in Hyûga had led to the apostacy of the leading Christian noblemen and to general rebellion in Bungo and its dependencies.

In view of this disastrous situation Valignano asked himself whether it would not be better to consolidate what had been gained rather than go on converting new masses of pagans, whom the insufficient number of missionaries could not properly instruct so as to safeguard them against falling back into paganism. On the other hand, he thought it would be a pity to let the chance of converting whole provinces slip away only because there were not enough missionaries to instruct them. Not knowing in which direction to move, Father Valignano asked the general of his order to decide the issue. He himself clearly indicated that he was inclined to push the work of conversion. Yet before he could hope to receive an answer from Rome, he had to make his own decision, as we shall see hereafter.

Another point which greatly harrassed Valignano was a lack of understanding of the Japanese and their culture on the part of the missionaries, particularly their superior, Father Cabral. He was a very zealous religious and an energetic leader, but he not only knew very little Japanese but was also of the opinion that Europeans could never learn it well enough to preach in public. Hence all preaching was to be done by Japanese helpers. Instead of winning their sympathy, Cabral treated them harshly, and even with contempt, insulting them. Those few whom he received into his order were not treated with kindness like their European brethren but with severity, for he feared that otherwise they would rebel against their foreign masters. For the same reason none of them was to be promoted to the priesthood or even admitted to higher studies. Instead of adapting himself to the way of life and the rules of courtesy of the Japanese, Cabral despised the Japanese and their culture and demanded of his native helpers an adaptation to European manners. No wonder that they had very little love for their master and his Order. The Japanese novices had no ascetical training whatever, but from the first day were thrown into the work and often left to themselves in situations in which even the strongest would have called for protection. Nor were they given any higher education, because the former soldier thought it unnecessary. It was easy to see that under such circumstances the Society of Jesus in Japan and its flourishing mission were doomed.

New Policy Outlined

If Valignano had been perplexed yet hesitated making any decision for improving this desperate situation, his remarkable success in Arima so enhanced his courage that he took the first steps to bring about a change for the better. He drew up a set of rules and principles for the superior of the mission which demanded that he govern his subjects in the spirit of love and sympathy. European and Japanese members of the Order were to be treated alike in every respect. To remedy the scarcity of missionaries many Japanese were to be received into the order, given a thorough ascetical training, admitted to the higher studies of philosophy and theology and finally promoted to holy orders. The European missionaries were to study the language of the country, adapt themselves to the Japanese way of life and, above all, know and strictly observe the Japanese rules of courtesy. A novitiate was to be erected for the spiritual training of the aspirants to the order; likewise a college of Japanese and scientific training for the young members, and seminaries for the education of boys who were thought fit to become some day useful helpers as catechists or priests.

To facilitate the administration of the immense mission, the whole territory was to be divided into three regions: Shimo, northwestern Kyûshû; Bungo, eastern Kyûshû and western Honshû; and Miyako, central Japan. Each district was to have a regional superior who was to visit every residence and station once a year. The general superior of the mission was to visit every house at least once in three years.

Father Valignano himself started a seminary at Arima shortly after the conversion of Harunobu and gave orders to Father Organtino to erect a second one in the Miyako district. Organtino at once assembled the building materials in Kyôto, but since he could not find a proper site in the capital, the materials were shipped to Azuchi, Nobunaga's new residence, and the edifice put up on the plot which Nobunaga had donated to Father Organtino for the erection of a church. Thus during the summer of 1580 two seminaries were established, but the third was never erected.

Valignano's views were by no means shared by Father Cabral. He voiced his complete disagreement and was convinced that Valignano was wrong. When therefore the Macao ship brought bad news from India, he strongly advised the former to return to India without visiting either Bungo or central Japan. In this way he hoped that things would remain as they had been before. Valignano resolved to stay and to carry out his program. He was to no small extent influenced in this resolution by the entreaties of Father Organtino to visit the district of Miyako. It was good luck for the Japanese mission that the Visitor did go to Bungo and Miyako.

In Bungo Father Valignano was greatly impressed by the heroic figure of Ôtomo Sôrin, who in spite of all misfortunes and contradictions remained firm in his Christian convictions. It was he who most strongly insisted on a thorough adaptation to the Japanese way of life, and upon his advice, Valignano drew up a set of rules of courtesy to which all missionaries were bound. A novitiate was opened at Usuki and a college at Funai—the Ôita of today—during Valignano's stay in Bungo.

In the spring of 1581 the Visitor set out for Gokinai. The celebration of Holy Week and Easter at Takatsuki greatly impressed him. Here he saw men like Takayama Ukon, Ikeda Tango-no-Kami, Yûki Yaheiji and Joam Yûki, men who had embraced the Christian faith out of personal conviction and without any hope for temporal gain and who were model Christians and apostles to their subjects. The masses of faithful flocking together from Kyôto and the neighboring cities and their genuine piety convinced the Visitor that the Japanese were capable of becoming good Christians and that Japan was the most important mission of the Society of Jesus.

In Kyôto Father Valignano was received in audience by Nobunaga and was greatly honored; still greater honors awaited him at Azuchi. Nobunaga's greatest favor was the donation of a beautiful screen of Azuchi Castle, which he had refused to give to even the Emperor Ôgimachi.

As a result of Nobunaga's favors the Japanese lords vied to honor the Jesuit Visitor, and when he returned to Bungo, all his doubts had disappeared. The work of evangelization was to go on vigorously, the friendship of princes to be fostered and the conversion of entire provinces to be pushed. The only obstacle to Valignano's policy was Father Cabral, who would not change his views and had even asked the general to relieve him of his office, since he could not accept principles which he believed to be wrong. Valignano, realizing that under such circumstances a change in the direction of the mission was imperative, relieved Father Cabral of his office and Father Gaspar Coelho replaced him. Until then the Japanese mission had been a dependency of the Province of India, but the new superior was to be Vice-Provincial of Japan, that is, head of a practically independent Vice-Province which, for the time being, had still to rely on the Province of India for material support and new helpers.

Before returning to India Father Valignano inaugurated an embassy of the three Christian *daimyô* of Kyûshû (Bungo, Arima and Ômura) to the Papal Court. They were to give homage to the Vicar of Christ and ask his support for the seminaries just erected, which were of such capital importance for the future of the Japanese mission.

Valignano himself had hoped to introduce the embassy to His Holiness, but when he reached Goa he learned that he had been appointed Provincial of India. Thus he had to stay there and charged Father Mesquita to lead the ambassadors to Europe.

VII

The Church under Hideyoshi's Rule

Nobunaga's Assassination

Less than five months after Father Valignano had left Japan, Nobunaga fell a victim to his treacherous general, Akechi Mitsuhide. Although he had not withdrawn his favor from the missionaries during his last five months, the Fathers were greatly shocked by his blasphemous ambition of divine worship. On the Azuchi castle hill he had built a magnificent temple, the object of worship being nothing less than himself. Great favors were promised to those, who would worship the "living god" in his new sanctuary, and only too many responded to his impious call. Before one month had elapsed after the dedication of Nobunaga's temple, he was struck down by the dagger of the traitor. Father Frois, who has left us a telling account of the tragedy, sees in Nobunaga's sudden death an act of heavenly justice.

Nobunaga's death caused war and chaos. Nobunaga's eldest son, Nobutada, had been slain, and his younger brothers, Nobuo and Nobutaka, could not agree who was to receive the heritage of their father. Ambitious generals fostered the fratricidal strife so as to secure a rich inheritance for themselves. If Akechi had hoped to succeed his victim, he was soon disillusioned. He was defeated by Nobunaga's most capable general, Hideyoshi, and subsequently killed by the peasants for the sake of his armor. In the course of the following wars Hideyoshi came out victorious. To legitimatize his claim to the rule of Japan he had himself invested with the office of *kampaku* or regent by Emperor Ôgimachi and was thus made the actual ruler of Japan.

Takayama Ukon's Apostolate

Hideyoshi like his predecessor favored Christianity. He even chose his favorites from among the Christian lords. Takayama Ukon was made chief of his bodyguard; Konishi Yukinaga, his grand admiral; Yukinaga's father, Ryûsa, his treasurer and governor of the great commercial city of Sakai; and Ai Ryôchi, his secretary. Takayama Ukon, undoubtedly the leader of the Christians of Gokinai, availed himself of Hideyoshi's favor for the benefit of Christianity. He asked the *kampaku* to donate land for a church from his new residence at Ôsaka and Hideyoshi agreed. He then suggested that the abandoned church of Okayama, in Kawachi, be transfered to Ôsaka.

This lovely church was in some danger of becoming a pagan temple. Since the Christian *samurai* went off with their lord, Yûki, the year before to Sangajima—because of the Christian Sanga's alliance with Akechi Mitsuhide—there were scarcely any Christians left in Okayama. Ukon wanted to save the church from profanation and simultaneously make it serve a real function in Hideyoshi's residence at Ôsaka. Takayama himself agreed to assume the expenses and at Christmas time, 1583, Ôsaka had a fine church.

Takayama not only enjoyed Hideyoshi's favor but also, due to his charming personality, had many friends among the lords. His popularity helped him draw a number of his friends to the Church, the most outstanding of them being Gamô Ujisato and Kuroda Yoshitaka. Both of them became great lay-apostles. With Konishi Yukinaga they began a vigorous apostolate among the *daimyô* and *samurai*. Takayama advised his friends to listen to the sermons in the new church and, since he was considered a model of chilvary, it was but natural that his appeal drew crowds to the church. Eventually

111

it became quite the fashion to listen to the sermons and a great many of the noble rank asked for baptism. Among the most illustrious converts were Hideyoshi's physician, Manase Dôsan, and Nobunaga's second son, Oda Nobuo.

The greatest number of converts were made by Takayama in his fief of Takatsuki. Since 1573 it had doubled both in size and population. Though the number of Christians had been growing rapidly as a result of the zeal of both Ukon and his father, there were, in 1582, vestiges of paganism. After Nobunaga's death, Ukon succeeded in leading the entire population of about 30,000 to the faith.

Since Azuchi was burned and abandoned after Nobunaga's death the Jesuit seminary had to be moved to a more central location. For a time it was transfered to Kyôto but the tiny church plot was too small to accommodate the large community. Takayama constructed a new seminary at Takatsuki and when he himself was transfered to Akashi in 1585 the seminary was moved to Ôsaka.

Hideyoshi Turns Persecutor

As has been stated above, since 1578 the Christian Ôtomos of Bungo had been much harassed by the powerful Shimazus of Kagoshima. At first the Shimazus were allied with Ryûzôji Takanobu of Saga but when he became too powerful they made peace with the Ôtomos through Nobunaga and devoted their energies toward the destruction of Ryûzôji. In 1584 at Shimabara the latter was defeated and killed by the combined forces of the Shimazus and the Christian, Arima Harunobu.

Meanwhile, in Bungo and its dependencies, Ôtomo Sôrin, who had at the request of his nobles temporarily resumed the reins of a government badly handled by his incapable son, Yoshimune, had restored order and peace to a certain extent. His unshakeable faith despite all adversity not only gave new courage to the Christians but also drew a large number of pagans to the Church.

Before Sôrin's baptism in 1587 there were no more than 2,500 Christians in Bungo, but at the end of the following year their number had risen to 6,000 and continued rising. In 1585 alone, 12,000 received baptism and in the following year, 3,000 more. In 1587 there were in Bungo at least 30,000 Christians.

The above is the figure given by the Vice-Provincial Coelho. His successor, Pedro Gomez, gives a figure twice as high. Gomez probably included those who postponed their conversion because of the general upheaval and lack of missionaries. We know the entire population of Paul Shiga's fief, some 40,000, were willing to become Christian.

When the Shimazus had destroyed Ryûzôji they

again turned against the Ôtomos, aiming at nothing less than a domination of the entire island of Kyû- shû. Ôtomo Yoshimune, who had again resumed the administration of the Bungo fief, saw that the only way to save his land was by asking Hideyoshi to help him against his powerful enemy. At this time the Vice-Provincial of the Jesuits, Father Coelho, was planning a visit to the *kampaku* to thank him for the many favors bestowed on Chris- tianity. At the same time he intended to prepare the ground for Ôtomo Sôrin's call so as to make sure that his request would be granted. Shimazu Yoshihisa, who knew of Father Coelho's plans, threatened him if he were to go to Ôsaka before the end of the year, because he hoped to have finished with the Ôtomos by that time.

Father Coelho complied with Shimazu's request to a certain extent but, nevertheless, proceeded to Ôsaka before Yoshihisa had completely routed his enemy. Hideyoshi received the Vice-Provincial with great courtesy, and Coelho, who naively be- lieved the crafty lord's flatteries, became unduly involved in the political turmoil to the great chargin of Father Organtino and the Christian lords, particularly Takayama Ukon.

When a short time later Ôtomo Sôrin called on Hideyoshi, he was received with open arms. Hide- yoshi had been waiting for his appeal for it gave him a welcome opportunity to extend his sway over Kyûshû. Presently he ordered Shimazu Yoshihisa to halt his war of conquest, but was not obeyed. Hence he resolved to lead a powerful army against Kyûshû the following year. Before Hideyoshi's arrival Yoshihisa had conquered nearly all the dependencies of the Ôtomos and even invaded their home province. To check further advances Hideyoshi had dispatched Kuroda Yoshitaka, who successfully challenged the enemy and reconquered a part of the lost territory. When at last Hideyoshi arrived with the main force it was only a matter of weeks before the Shimazus were compelled to capitulate without even a serious encounter in the field.

The war over, Hideyoshi proceeded to the little town of Hakozaki to redistribute the provinces of Kyûshû according to his own will. The Shimazus were confined to the provinces of Satsuma and Ôsumi and a part of Hyûga; the Ôtomos had to content themselves with their home province of Bungo; the Christian lords of Ômura, Amakusa and Arima were guaranteed the possession of their petty fiefs; and the Christian Itôs recovered a part of their province of Hyûga. The Christian general, Kuroda Yoshitaka, received the better part of Buzen and the Christian, Môri Hidekane, was given a large fief in the province of Chikugo. In short, nearly one half of the island of Kyûshû was in the hands of Christian lords and the outlook for the spread of Christianity seemed very promising. During the campaign Hideyoshi had received Father Coelho in audience at Yatsushiro and at his request had granted life and freedom to the garrison of the doomed fortress. He, moreover, invited the Vice-Provincial to meet him again after the war at Hakata.

Father Coelho, who for safe travelling had at his disposal a well-armed ship, was imprudent enough to come to Hakata with it. He was received with the customary courtesy by the *kampaku* and hence was full of optimism for the future of the mission. Many lords came to see his ship and so greatly praised and admired its excellent armament that Hideyoshi also paid a visit to Coelho to have a look at the wonderful craft. He did not mince words in its praise to Father Coelho's great satisfaction. When Takayama Ukon and Konishi Yukinaga heard of it, they were struck with fear and urged Coelho to offer the ship to Hideyoshi as a present, since otherwise all was lost. This the naive Father was unable to understand and stubbornly refused to do.

At the same time an unusually large Portuguese ship had arrived at Hirado and Hideyoshi sent word to the captain through Coelho that he should sail to Hakata, since he wanted to see the ship. The captain believed it to be too risky to steer the large vessel through the shallow waters of Hakata Bay, but, in order not to offend Hideyoshi, he came himself to Hakata to apologize. Apparently Hideyoshi was convinced of the plausibility of his apology, yet on that very night he turned persecutor.

Numberless explanations have been given for this sudden change of policy, but none of them satisfies completely. Was it Coelho's imprudent meddling in politics or his well-armed ship that had aroused Hideyoshi's suspicion, or was his vanity offended by the captain's refusal to bring his ship to Hakata, or was Hideyoshi's favor to Christianity nothing but a clever mask, which he at last could throw off because he no longer needed the services of the Christian lords and the missionaries? His real motives may perhaps never be fully understood, but there is ample evidence that for many years he had entertained suspicions about the activity of the missionaries and that it was expressly fostered by his physician, the ex-bonze Seyakuin Sensô, a bitter enemy of Christianity and a personal foe of Takayama Ukon. On that fatal night this dangerous man (Father Frois tells us), resentful of a personal embarrassment, violently charged the missionaries with ambitious plans and accused the Christian lords, particularly Takayama

The Catholic Church in Japan

Ukon, of being their allies. Hideyoshi, already half-intoxicated with the Portuguese wine which Coelho had sent him, was aroused to such a fit of anger that he at once sent orders to Takayama that he should give up his faith or else be deposed and sent abroad into exile.

Ukon's chivalrous answer was that he would give up his faith for nothing in the world and that he would consider it an honor to suffer exile for his Christian conviction. Thereupon Hideyoshi deposed him but did not expel him from the country. Simultaneously the missionaries received strict orders to leave Japan within twenty days.

Hideyoshi's Edict Ignored

If Hideyoshi had been determined to carry out his edict, Christianity would have been doomed. As a matter of fact, he was not and things remained much the same as they had been before. He did attempt to make the Christian lords of Arima and Ômura apostatize but failed. Perhaps he had expressly waited with his prohibition until Ômura Sumitada and Ôtomo Sôrin, the two columns of the Church, had died, and although the cowardly Ôtomo Yoshimune apostatized and even killed a number of Christians, Sumitada's son, Yoshisaki, showed himself worthy of his valiant father. Orders were given to tear down the churches of Arima and Ômura, but

The Church under Hideyoshi's Rule

the Christian lords found ways and means of delaying the execution, and when Hideyoshi left Kyûshû soon after, no more churches were destroyed. Father Coelho had declared to Hideyoshi that it would be impossible to find transportation for so many within twenty days and the *kampaku* extended the days of grace to six months but insisted that all missionaries should assemble at Hirado to await deportation.

In Gokinai the work of evangelization came to a standstill, but in Kyûshû there was little change, except that the Fathers donned the Japanese *kimono* and proceeded with great caution and moderation. Their forced leisure was even an advantage, since now they were able to instruct their neophytes properly. Only a few of the missionaries left the country, but they were distributed to the fiefs of the Christian lords where they could take care of their Christians and even make a good number of converts. Hideyoshi had seized and subsequently destroyed the churches of Kyôto, Ôsaka and Sakai, but the Christians were consoled by the letters and occasional visits of Father Organtino from his safe hiding place on Shôdoshima in the Inland Sea. In the midst of the turmoil of persecution the Church made one of the greatest of her converts, the famous Gracia Hosokawa, wife of the brave general, Hosokawa Tadaoki. Hideyoshi knew that the Fathers had remained in Japan but he dissimulated because he feared that the Macao ships would no longer come to Japan if he insisted on the deportation of the missionaries.

Valignano's Embassy to Hideyoshi

During the last days of May, 1587, the Japanese envoys to the Holy See landed at Goa. They had been received with great enthusiasm by the King of Spain, the Pope and the Italian princes. They had brought with them valuable presents and also a printing press, which was to turn out the first books with movable type in Japan. When the envoys arrived at Goa the persecution had not as yet started in Japan.

The Vice-Provincial's courteous reception at Ôsaka and Hideyoshi's numerous other favors had prompted Father Coelho to suggest an embassy from the Viceroy of India to the *kampaku* to thank him for all he had done for the Church. Valignano thereupon proposed that he himself should go as ambassador and simultaneously introduce the four envoys at Hideyoshi's court. The Viceroy gladly consented to this proposal because the presents brought from Europe were to be offered to the *kampaku* in his own name.

When, in the spring of 1588, Valignano arrived with the four envoys at Macao he learned of Hide-

yoshi's anti-Christian policy and as a result even
more eagerly insisted on carrying out the plan
of the embassy. Hideyoshi was consulted as to
whether he would accept the homage and at once
consented. In early summer, 1590, Valignano landed at Nagasaki, but not until the spring of 1591
was he received in solemn audience by Hideyoshi.
Enemies of the Church had not failed to denounce
Valignano's embassy as spurious, asserting that he
had never left Japan and hoped to rehabilitate the
missionaries by means of a fake embassy. Although
the ambassador was unable to obtain the cancella-
tion of the edict of exile, his visit had, nevertheless,
a number of happy consequences for the mission.
Ten priests were allowed to remain at Nagasaki,
technically for the benefit of the Portugese crew
of the Macao ships, but in reality to take care of the
Japanese Christians as well.

The young Jesuit João Rodriguez had found
grace in Hideyoshi's eyes and was employed as his
official interpreter so that he could move freely
about the country. The aged Father Organtino was
allowed to live in Kyôto; Hideyoshi was moved to
pity because of his old age. Thus it became possible
to resume the work of evangelization in Gokinai,
although no church could be built. Hideyoshi's
familiar intercourse with the Portuguese in Kyûshû
resulted in a craze of imitation of Portuguese dress

and customs. It became fashionable to wear reliquaries and crosses, and we are told that even Hideyoshi did the same, although officially he had prohibited Christianity and all its manifestations.

Remarkable Progress

In Kyûshû despite Hideyoshi's prohibition, the work of evangelization had been progressing vigorously since 1587 particularly in Amakusa, Arima and Gotô. From 1593 to 1596 Father Organtino carried on an apostolate among the great lords of Gokinai which in its results eclipsed even the prosperous years of the Ôsaka period, 1583-1587. Among the best known converts were Oda Hidenobu, Nobunaga's grandson and heir apparent; his younger brother; the two eldest sons of the governor of Kyôto, Maeda Munehisa, as well as two of his nephews; several members of the illustrious Ukita family, which governed the three provinces of Bizen, Bitchû and Mimasaka; and the younger brother of Hosokawa Tadaoki, Hosokawa Okimoto. Takayama Ukon had again been admitted to Hideyoshi's favor, and although he did not again become a ruling *daimyô,* he nevertheless made many converts among the great lords and even induced Maeda Toshinaga, eldest son of his suzerain, Maeda Toshiie, to consider the acceptance of Christianity.

Even before Father Valignano's second arrival

The Church under Hideyoshi's Rule

in Japan a son of Emperor Goyôzei with his entire
family had embraced Christianity. Terazawa Hirotaka, since 1592 governor of Nagasaki, was changed
from a bitter enemy into a friend and finally a convert to Christianity. In 1587 the number of Christians was estimated at about 200,000 and ten years
later it had risen to nearly 300,000. Thus in spite
of Hideyoshi's persecution the faith spread rapidly
and the Christians were left entirely unmolested.

The 26 Martyrs of Nagasaki

The progress and peace of the Church were
suddenly interrupted by a sanguinary persecution
which threatened her very existence. In 1591
Hideyoshi at the suggestion of a Christian adventurer, Paul Harada Kiemon, had sent a haughty
letter to the governor of the Philippines in which
he demanded an oath of vassalage. The governor,
pretending not fully to understand the meaning of
the letter, sent the Dominican Juan Cobo to Japan
as ambassador. The outcome of the negotiations is
not known for sure since Cobo was shipwrecked
and thrown among the barbarians of Formosa.
Shortly after Cobo's departure from Japan, Harada
Kiemon went on his own accord to the Philippines
and urged the governor to send Franciscans to
Japan under the plea that Hideyoshi would receive
them kindly. He was by no means hostile to

Christianity as such, said Harada; he disliked only the Jesuits. In vain the Jesuits at Manila pointed out that according to a brief of Pope Gregory XIII all non-Jesuits were prohibited under pain of excommunication from work in Japan.

During his first visit to Japan, Father Valignano had discussed with the Fathers the question of whether friars from the Philippines ought to be called to Japan because of the scarcity of workers in the mission field. The majority of Fathers, as well as Valignano, despite this urgent need, were of the opinion that because of the suspicious attitude of the bonzes and the non-Christian lords, and in view of greater uniformity of procedure, it would be better that for the moment no more Spanish friars should come to Japan. With this in mind Valignano sent a memorandum to Rome and asked for a prohibition of missionary activity by non-Jesuits. Thereupon Pope Gregory on January 28, 1585, issued the brief *Ex pastorali officio.*

The friars believed that under the circumstances this prohibition did not apply because of the urgent needs of the Japanese Christians and the essentially diplomatic character of the Franciscan mission. As a matter of fact, Father Pedro Bautista, O. F. M., with three other Franciscans, were sent as ambassadors to Hideyoshi in 1593.

It would lead too far afield to narrate all the

details of their audience but this much is certain: Father Pedro Bautista's firm stand so impressed the haughty Hideyoshi that he no longer insisted on the oath of vassalage on the part of the Manila governor. Instead he offered an alliance of friendship, invited Spanish ships to his ports and gave safe conduct to them. When Father Bautista asked to see Kyôto and stay there, Hideyoshi consented and subsequently donated a plot of land and even granted the Franciscans permission to build a convent "as they used to have them in Spain." Yet he did not give the Fathers a written document on his grant.

The Franciscans by their charitable work aroused the admiration of Christians and non-Christians. They opened a hospital in Kyôto, another in Ôsaka, and dispatched some friars to Nagasaki to establish a third hospital in that city. Since their propaganda was carried on quite openly they were warned by the Jesuits and even by the sympathetic governors of Kyôto to moderate their zeal and proceed with the utmost caution, but these warnings were not heeded, because the Franciscans honestly believed that they acted with Hideyoshi's express permission.

At the beginning of October, 1596, the *San Felipe* on her way from the Philippines to Mexico was stranded at Urado on the coast of Shikoku. The lord of the land, Chôsokabe Motochika, assured the captain of his sympathy and advised him to send an envoy with a present to Hideyoshi so as to obtain entrance to the Kyôto governor, Masuda Naga-mori, by whose good offices Hideyoshi would un-doubtedly grant all the captain desired. Before the captain's messengers set out for Gokinai the double-faced Motochika dispatched a courier to Masuda and urged him to prevail upon Hideyoshi to confiscate the rich booty as shipwreck, according to the laws of Japan. He pointed out that the *San Felipe* was armed, had ammunition on board and a number of priests among her passengers. When the captain's envoys arrived at Kyôto they were told to wait until the proper moment when Hideyoshi would accept their present and listen to their request. Meanwhile they were treated with the utmost courtesy by Masuda, in whose mansion they stopped. According to strict orders of the captain, the envoy had notified Father Bautista of what was going on and asked for his help.

After a few days Masuda told Father Bautista that Hideyoshi could not accept the captain's pre-sent because he had not offered it in person. As a matter of fact the captain had intended to go him-self to Kyôto, but Chôsokabe had dissuaded him from doing so. Very soon the Father learned that Hideyoshi had sent Masuda to Urado to confiscate ship and cargo. Thereupon Father Bautista prevailed upon the friendly governor, Maeda Munehisa, to present to Hideyoshi the text of his passport for Spanish ships to make him realize that the confiscation of the *San Felipe* was a breach of his solemn pledge. Hideyoshi was greatly embarrassed but was too proud to cancel his order. To save face he had to find another pretext to justify his order. It will be remembered how Chôsokabe Motochika in his letter to Masuda Nagamori had pointed out that the *San Felipe* was armed and had priests on board. From this it might be possible to prove that the *San Felipe* had come to Japan to attack the country and to use the priests as spies for the conquest of Japan. Presently Hideyoshi sent a courier to Masuda, told him of his embarrassment and probably pointed to the solution of the dilemma. Among other things he wrote that the *San Felipe* had come to Japan to conquer the land and that three years before Franciscans had been sent to prepare the way, that this had happened in the conquest of Mexico, Peru and the Philippines.

Masuda understood Hideyoshi's hint and cleverly set out to substantiate his charge. It goes without saying that the Spaniards at Urado strongly protested against the confiscation of their ship, and, as a matter of fact, the pilot did not fail to boast

of the power of the Spanish king. On a sea chart
he showed Masuda the enormous colonial empire
of his king, insinuating that it was dangerous to
challenge such a mighty monarch. Thereupon
Masuda wanted to know how the Spaniards had
succeeded in conquering so many distant lands.
The pilot replied that they traded with the peoples
of the whole world, and if they were well received
they behaved as friends, but if they were treated
badly, they would seize the land. To this Masuda
replied: "And for this reason the Fathers must
come first?" The perplexed pilot answered: "Yes."

Of all the many accounts of this episode the
foregoing would seem to be the most plausible,
and there can be no doubt that the good pilot had
been cleverly trapped by the shrewd Masuda, who,
as it were, put the desired answer on his tongue.
Be that as it may, this much is certain: that the
San Felipe was confiscated as war booty and that
the Franciscan missionaries and their disciples
were put to death for having prepared the way for
the ill-fated ship, as clearly appears from the contemporary accounts of Luis Frois, S.J., and Pedro
Bautista, O.F.M. It is true that on the proclamation board their preaching of Christian doctrine
against Hideyoshi's prohibition was given as the
reason for their execution. The fact that Bautista
was overwhelmed with joy when at the place of

execution he for the first time heard that he was to die for preaching the Gospel is decisive proof that until then he had been under the painful impression that he was to be crucified on a political charge. The fact that Hideyoshi based his sentence on the disobedience of the Franciscans to his prohibition clearly shows that the Kyôto governors and the Jesuits were perfectly justified in warning the Franciscans to be on their guard and not to trust Hideyoshi's oral permission. Among the twenty-six victims there were three Japanese Jesuits. This was due to a misunderstanding which, had it been cleared up, would probably have had consequences fatal to the Church and brought about a general persecution.

The twenty-six martyrs were led to Nagasaki and crucified on Mount Tateyama on February 5, 1597. Subsequently an edict was issued to the effect that all missionaries, except a few for the ministration of the Portuguese merchants at Nagasaki, were to leave the country; some of them were actually deported to Macao. All the rest would undoubtedly have shared the same fate, had not Hideyoshi's death on September 16, 1598, changed the situation completely.

VIII

The Calm before the Storm

Mass Conversions

Hideyoshi left as heir his infant son, Hideyori. To make sure that the mightiest man in the country, Tokugawa Ieyasu, would be loyal to Hideyori, Hideyoshi made him the principal tutor of the boy and the head of the five regents. Although in this way Ieyasu was greatly honored his powers were, nevertheless, considerably limited by the more or less equal rights of his four colleagues on the board of regents. Nor could he neutralize their influence by arbitrary interpretation of the decrees of the regents, for a board of five ministers, the *bugyô,* was to see to it that they were promptly and faithfully carried out. In this way Hideyoshi had hoped to attach Ieyasu firmly to his cause and at the same time keep him in proper bounds until Hideyori would reach maturity.

The Catholic Church in Japan

A war with Korea had been dragging on for six years without either decisive results or the prospect of victory in the near future. Hence Hideyoshi before his death had given orders to recall the troops from Korea. In the early summer of 1598 Valignano had arrived for a third time in Japan. With him came Bishop Luis de Cerqueira. When Valignano learned that two members of the board of ministers were being sent to Korea he visited them at Hakata and announced his arrival. They assured him of their good will but at the same time advised the Fathers to proceed with great moderation and tact. Seeing the wisdom of their advice, the Fathers abstained from public activity for the rest of the year.

In the spring of the following year the governor of Nagasaki, Terazawa Hirotaka, who meanwhile had returned to paganism, began to harass the Christians and would not allow them to visit the church. Thereupon Father João Rodriguez visited Ieyasu and was kindly received. Ieyasu would not and could not comply with Rodriguez' request to annul Hideyoshi's anti-Christian laws, yet he sent word to Terazawa to abstain from unfriendly acts towards the Christians.

Scarcely was this difficulty solved when new trouble arose. The *daimyô* of Hirado, Matsura Shigenobu, had given orders to compel all Christians to take part in the solemn funeral of his father, Takanobu, and to make his Christian *samurai,* particularly the valiant Kotedas, apostatize. The Kotedas, resolved to stand by their faith, secretly left Hirado with 600 retainers and fled to Nagasaki, but Terazawa would not allow them to settle in the city. They found refuge in Ômura's land on the outskirts of Nagasaki. When Matsuura Shigenobu learned what had happened, he was furious and took every possible precaution to forestall a further exodus, but 200 more Christians managed to escape to Nagasaki. Thus, in the end, the Christians were left in peace.

Ieyasu's friendly reaction to Rodriguez' visit encouraged the Fathers as well as the Christian lords to engage in a more vigorous spreading of the faith. A good many non-Christian lords who sympathized with Christianity expressed the desire of having missionaries in their domains. As a result the missionary staff was reinforced in Hyûga, Chikugo, Tsushima and Isahaya and new missions established in Bungo, Buzen, in the fiefs of Môri Terumoto and Ukita Hideie and, above all, in southern Higo, the domain of Konishi Yukinaga. This valiant Christian had never wavered and nevertheless enjoyed Hideyoshi's favor but to his regret could not openly spread the Christian faith in his land lest he provoke the tyrant's anger. Now

133

at last he inaugurated a vigorous Christian propaganda in his fief with the result that in less than one year 30,000 baptisms were administered. Similar results were obtained in the other missions so that from the spring of 1599 to the fall of 1600 no less than 70,000 were received into the Church.

Civil War: 1600

It was easy to foresee that discord would soon arise between the regents and ministers. It showed itself between Ishida Mitsunari and Asano Nagamasa in Korea, who could not agree as to how the war was to be ended. The majority of the five regents and with them the minister Ishida Mitsunari charged Ieyasu with treason against Hideyori, and both sides endeavored to make allies. Ieyasu spared no efforts to win Konishi Yukinaga over to his side, but failed, for Konishi honestly believed that his friend Ishida Mitsunari was more loyal to Hideyori. And when Ieyasu demanded an oath of fidelity of all the *daimyô* Konishi swore with the reservation that it should not contradict his obligations to Hideyori. As a matter of fact, Konishi was, with Ishida, the soul of the league against Ieyasu.

At Sekigahara the armies engaged in a decisive battle. Although Ieyasu's enemies were far superior in numbers, he gained the victory, partly because of his military genius, partly because of the discord of his opponents and the treason of a number of their allies. Konishi and Ishida were made prisoners and subsequently executed by the victor. Of the great *daimyô* who had fought against Ieyasu, Ukita Hideie was deposed and exiled; Uesugi Kagekatsu, reduced to insignificance; Môri Terumoto, spoiled of the greater part of his domain; and Shimazu Yoshihiro, forced to resign. A number of Christian lords also felt the victor's wrath: Oda Hidenobu, Nobunaga's grandson, was deposed and exiled; Môri Hidekane and Amakusa Izu-no-Kami, stripped of their fiefs. Kuroda Yoshitaka and his son Nagamasa were the only Christian *daimyô* who had openly embraced Ieyasu's side. It was due to Yoshitaka's efforts that the lords of Arima and Ômura had remained neutral during the general turmoil and that they openly declared themselves for Ieyasu after the battle at Sekigahara. If Kuroda Yoshitaka had been lukewarm until shortly before the outbreak of the civil war, he had since regained his first fervor and acted like a true Christian prince during the struggle, and became the real protector of the Church after Konishi's downfall.

Konishi's siding with the enemy infuriated Ieyasu against Christianity. He maintained that it was an evil religion and taught its adherents to break their oaths. In this he was mistaken. Konishi had sworn him fidelity only in so far as it was compatible with his obligations toward Hideyoshi. Since he believed that Ieyasu was determined to push the latter aside he felt himself obliged to fight for the wronged child.

Ieyasu, unable to comprehend this logic, not only executed Konishi but also became very bitter toward Christianity which he held responsible for Konishi's "treason." It soon became evident who the real "traitor" was, however. In 1603, Ieyasu had himself invested *shôgun,* thus openly overruling Hideyori's legitimate claims and breaking the solemn oaths he had sworn at the deathbed of Hideyoshi.

It was to be feared that in view of his resentment against Christianity Ieyasu would start a violent persecution. This did not happen. On the contrary he even gave the Church a certain amount of freedom. The Jesuit churches at Kyôto, Ôsaka and Nagasaki as well as the Franciscan church at Edo were legally authorized, and no obstacles placed against Christian propaganda in the rest of the country. But this by no means meant that all danger had passed. Once when Ieyasu bitterly complained about Konishi's "treason" and threatened to expel all Fathers from the country, Terazawa pointed out that in Arima and Ômura there were many churches despite the express prohibition of the late Hideyoshi which the Christian *daimyô* had utterly disregarded. Terazawa was ordered to tear down all these churches, but Arima and Ômura declared that they would rather die than suffer this outrage on the part of their enemy. This bold language as well as the intercession of powerful friends induced Ieyasu to recall his order and legalize the churches of these Christian territories. He evidently realized that he was not as yet strong enough to challenge all the Christian lords and, morever, he was afraid that the Portuguese and Spanish vessels would stop coming to Japan if he were to start an open persecution. Thus he hid his anger for the time being and even granted a certain amount of freedom to both Jesuits and Franciscans, hoping to use their influence to attract foreign ships.

Ieyasu's apparent friendliness towards Christianity encouraged some of the most powerful non-Christian *daimyô* to favor and protect the Christians. One of them was Fukushima Masanori, who had received the two provinces of Aki and Bingo. In his capital of Hiroshima he donated a piece of land to the Church and was glad to see many of his retainers embrace Christianity. Hosokawa Tadaoki, greatly impressed by the funeral services which the Fathers held for his Christian wife, Gracia, who had met with a tragic death at the beginning of the civil war, became a warm friend of the Church and called the missionaries to his new capital of Kokura.

When Terazawa had succeeded Konishi Yukinaga as governer general of the coast districts of
northwestern Kyûshû and insisted that the Hirado
exiles should return to their native land, Hosokawa granted them hospitality and a liberal income
in his fief of Buzen. Even Terazawa, while realizing he was in danger of losing Ieyasu's favor,
thought it wise to make peace with the Fathers
and allow them to minister to his new subjects
of the Amakusa Archipelago.

Although Ieyasu had not entirely revoked
Hideyoshi's anti-Christian laws, the Church now
enjoyed greater freedom than at any time since the
outbreak of Hideyoshi's persecution. In Kyûshû,
above all, it had at last become possible to profess
the Christian religion without restraint and to display the sacred liturgy in all its splendor. Although
Bishop Cerquira had resided at Nagasaki from
1598, it was only in 1601 that for the first time he
could celebrate a pontifical High Mass. In the same
year he began to recruit a secular clergy, and on
September 22, 1601, he promoted the first Japanese
to the priesthood: the Jesuits Sebastian Kimura and
Luis Niabara. In 1605 the first public procession
was held at Nagasaki on the feast of Corpus Christi
to the great satisfaction of the Christian population.

It will be recalled that the four envoys to Europe

had brought with them a printing press with movable type. At Goa it turned out its first volume, a Latin discourse of Martin Hara, one of the envoys. At Macao, where Valignano had to wait two years for passage to Japan, two Latin prints were turned out by the press: *Christiani pueri institutio* by Juan Bonifacio, in 1588, and *De missione legatorum Iaponesium,* composed by Valignano from the journals of the envoys and translated by Durate de Sande into Latin, 1589-1590. In Japan the press was set up first at Katsusa, where a *Life of Saints* was printed in 1591 in Japanese but with Latin letters. About the same time prayer prints as well as a catechism, *Doctrina,* were printed with Japanese characters in wooden type. Thus the first type prints in Japan were turned out by the missionaries. The press had to be moved several times because of Hideyoshi's persecution, first to Amakusa, from 1592 to 1597, and finally to Nagasaki, from 1597 to 1611.

The first Latin type had been brought from Europe but Japanese mechanics very soon leaned to cast various kinds of type so that the mission became independent of the necessity of imports from Europe. The first Japanese type had been cut in wood, but only a few years later metal type was exclusively used, at the latest in 1598. The number of prints must have been considerable and the editions very large, since the books were distributed free of charge to the Christians. Apart from the works printed at Goa and Macao twenty-seven works of the Jesuit press in Japan have come down to us, and about the same number of other prints are known from the sources. If we bear in mind that all Christian objects were searched for and systematically destroyed in the raids of the long persecution, we may safely conclude that many more items than we know of today must have been turned out by the Jesuit press. Only very few prints escaped the raiders, and the majority of the few which are extant had been sent to friends in Europe and were thus saved from destruction. The latest Jesuit print we know of is dated Nagasaki, 1611, but it is certain the press must have been working three years longer for only in 1614 was it moved to Macao.

Mediocre Progress

After Ieyasu had risen to power Japan enjoyed its most profound peace since the arrival of Saint Francis Xaxier. As a result missionary activity went on undisturbed, whereas in former years the fruit of long and tireless labor was often destroyed by a single political catastrophe. Yet in spite of peace and stability the number of converts was much smaller than even during the ten years of

Hideyoshi's persecution. According to the statistics of the annual letters the yearly baptisms were between only 5,000 and 7,000, although since 1602 not only Jesuits and Franciscans but also Dominicans and Augustinians and soon after a number of Japanese secular priests were engaged in missionary activity.

The main reason for such meagre results was the strict prohibition of baptism to the noble classes. Hideyoshi had also issued a similar prohibition but did not strictly insist on its enforcement, whereas Ieyasu was firmly resolved to enforce it to the very letter. The fact that since 1600 no single ruling *daimyô* had the courage openly to receive baptism is a clear proof that Ieyasu meant what he said. Kyôgoku Takatsugu became a Christian, probably due to the entreaties of his pious mother, Maria, and his younger brother, Takamoto; yet he was baptized in strictest secrecy and carefully kept his secret. Even men like Hosokawa Tadaoki and Fukushima Masanori, who had the highest respect for the Christian faith and even urged their retainers to adopt it, did not even for a moment consider becoming Christians themselves, because they feared incurring Ieyasu's wrath. Hosokawa's son and heir, Tadatoshi, who greatly cherished the memory of his heroic mother, Gracia, and was in his heart a Christian, did not receive baptism out of fear of Ieyasu's prohibition. Maeda Toshinaga, the mighty lord of the three provinces of Kaga, Etchû and Noto, as early as 1591 had expressed his determination of becoming a Christian, but he never had the courage to carry out his resolution.

During the first fifty years of the Japanese mission time and again mass conversions had occurred, but they happened only when a ruling *daimyô* became Christian. Hence from 1600 on there were no more mass conversions for the simple reason that no ruling *daimyô* had the courage to embrace the faith. With regard to the *samurai* class Ieyasu's prohibition was not so strictly enforced but, nevertheless, it kept the number of converts within modest bounds.

Apart from Ieyasu's prohibition the precarious legal status of the Church was a great obstacle to a vigorous expansion of the Christian faith. After the battle of Sekigahara, Ieyasu legalized only the churches of Kyôto, Ôsaka, Nagasaki and Edo and a little later all the churches of Arima and Ômura. As a result, in the rest of the country the work of evangelization was, at least technically, illegal and, at the best, only tolerated. Hence any church, apart from those formally legalized, could be suppressed at any time without a new enactment or ordinance . As a matter of fact, the Franciscan and Jesuit churches in Kyôto were actually suppressed before the beginning of the general persecution.

Ieyasu's occasional anti-Christian outbursts and policies were another reason why many were deterred from embracing Christianity. When, in 1602, Franciscans, Dominicans and Augustinians came from the Philippines to work in the Japanese mission field, Ieyasu was greatly exasperated and threatened to destroy Christianity, because he was disappointed that, instead of Spanish ships, Spanish friars had arrived. When somewhat later he was told that there were a number of Christians in Hideyori's service, he issued a decree to the effect that no Christian was to serve the young prince. Although the Christians for a time dreaded a persecution in the Ôsaka district, nothing happened. When a similar charge was made at Edo, a careful investigation was ordered and a very strict prohibition of the reception of baptism issued. When not as many ships from the Philippines came to Ieyasu's ports as he had expected, the Spanish missionaries were penalized.

Local Persecutions

Despite the profound peace in the country and the comparative freedom granted to the Christians, there occurred time and again persecutions instigated by lords hostile to Christianity. Katô Kiyomasa, *daimyô* of northern Higo, as a result of his siding with Ieyasu in the civil war of 1600, had received the southern half of Higo, the fief of the unfortunate Konishi Yukinaga.

Since Katô had been for many years the main enemy of Konishi, the Christians of southern Higo could expect of him nothing but violent persecution. Through the good offices of Kuroda Yoshitaka it seemed, at least for a time, as if Katô would change his anti-Christian attitude. He even promised to grant the Christians the same privileges as they had enjoyed under his Christian predecessor. As a result, many of Konishi's retainers took service under the new lord. Yet Katô did not keep his promise and very soon began a cruel persecution.

The Christians were urged under terrible threats to apostatize, and, as the majority of them had only recently been baptized, a great many gave up their new religion as fast and as easily as they had adopted it. Konishi's former retainers, however, would not yield to any pressure and were thrown into jail. Through the intercession of outside friends they were finally set at liberty and allowed to leave the country. Others, particularly *samurai* and church-elders, gave their lives for their faith. No priest or catechist was allowed to live in Higo, although occasionally a missionary would secretly visit the abandoned flock and console and fortify them in their faith.

The Calm before the Storm

The church of Yamaguchi, which shortly after the departure of Saint Francis Xavier had been left without pastors until 1586 and again from 1587 to 1599, once more had to walk the Way of the Cross. It will be recalled how Môri Terumoto in 1600 had lost all his lands but the provinces of Suô and Nagato. The Môri family had always been greatly attached to Buddhism and for this reason had harassed the Christians and expelled the missionaries. The misfortunes of this great family in 1600 were attributed by the bonzes to the presence of the Fathers in its lands, so that it was not difficult for them to prevail upon their lord to oust them from Yamaguchi. Nor did he stop at this but in 1605 killed one of his principal retainers, the valiant Melchior Kumagaya, with ten members of his family, for being unwilling to apostatize. Another of his victims was the blind Damian, who for many years had ministered to the Christians and replaced the Fathers as best he could. Two more Christians were martyred at Hagi.

The Matsuras of Hirado from the very beginning had been hostile to Christianity and, if they abstained from the worst, it was because one of their first retainers, Antonio Koteda, was a fearless Christian and a brave soldier. The Matsuras had been at war for many years with the Ômuras, and when peace was finally concluded, a marriage

between Micia, a daughter of Ômura Sumitada, and
Matsura Hisanobu, grandson of Matsura Takanobu,
was to consolidate it. When, in 1599, Hisanobu's
father, Shigenobu, attempted to force the Christians
to take part in his father's funeral, Micia was also
urged to give up her faith, but she remained firm
and threatened to return to her brother, Ômura
Yoshisaki, rather than apostatize. In the end her
husband prevailed upon his father to let her live in
peace. As has been seen above, on this occasion
the Kotedas with 800 retainers went into voluntary
exile and, as a result, the remaining Christians lost
their main support. Micia's husband, however,
was friendly towards Christianity, allowed his wife
to baptize her children and even gave reason to
hope that he himself would become a Christian.
In any event, he protected the Christians against
his father. Unfortunately he died in 1602 and the
situation again became very bad for the poor
Christians. In 1609 and 1610 a number of Christians, among them three children, were killed for
the sake of their faith.

Another bitter enemy of Christianity was the
apostate Terazawa. If he abstained from violent
persecution it was only because he feared depopula-
ting his entirely Christian domain of Amakusa. He,
nevertheless, time and again harassed his Christian
subjects, hoping in this way to win back Ieyasu's

favor whenever he had reason to fear that he was losing it. Thus in 1604 he exiled from Amakusa 600 Christians, and in Karatsu he dismissed 70 Christians from his service. In Amakusa, moreover, he tore down all churches except two, cut down all crosses and urged the Christians to apostatize, but since they remained firm, he changed his policy and even tried to win back the friendship of the missionaries by leaving the Christians in peace.

Sources of Danger

The rapid progress of the mission until 1600 was to no small extent due to Nobunaga's and Hideyoshi's harsh treatment of the great Buddhist sects. Before Nobunaga's rise to power the disciples of Buddha had been a constant menace to the young Church, as appears most clearly in the troubled beginnings of the mission of Kyôto. If Nobunaga so conspicuously favored Christianity, it was partly because of his hatred of the bonzes, who persecuted the Christians. The destruction of the great monastery of Hieizan and the conquest of the Honganji stronghold of Ôsaka greatly humiliated and weakened the Buddhists, and Hideyoshi's war of annihilation against the bonzes of Negorodera added to their plight. With the ascendency of Ieyasu, however, the situation was radically changed. The new ruler of Japan was an ardent Buddhist and his fervor increased as he grew older. As a result, Buddhism again began to assert itself and to become once more a danger to Christianity, all the more so as Ieyasu used the bonzes as advisers in his policy towards Christianity.

Apart from Buddhism, Confucianism and *Shintô* also became a menace to Christianity. To meet the danger of these three national religions the Jesuit Fabian Fukan composed a dialogue, *Myôtei Mondô,* in which he refuted Buddhism, Confucianism and *Shintô* and defended Christianity, of which he gave a summary in the last part of the dialogue. In 1606 Fabian had a public disputation with Hayashi Razan or Dôshun, the most outstanding Neo-Confucianist of the 17th century. The result was that Hayashi became even more hostile to Christianity. This was all the more fatal since he played an ever growing part in shaping the Tokugawa policy towards Christianity and, in 1608, became librarian and secretary of the shôgunate.

It is noteworthy that the revival of national *Shintô* received its inspiration from the renaissance of Confucianism of the 17th century. Since the Tokugawa were eagerly concerned in maintaining and strengthening the unification of the country, which had been brought about by the successive efforts of the three great national heroes, Nobunaga, Hideyoshi and Ieyasu, it is but natural that the emphasis of the national religions in opposition to the foreign creed fitted their aims and became an important factor in firmly establishing their rule.

Perhaps the greatest of all dangers which threatened Christianity was the appearance of the Dutch and the English on the scene. In 1600 the Dutch ship *De Liefde* was driven aground on the coast of Bungo. Among the few survivors of the stranded ship was the pilot, William Adams, an Englishman. The entire crew was interned, and the Portuguese, greatly alarmed at the appearance of prospective rivals for the profitable trade monopoly they had enjoyed for so many years, urged Ieyasu to punish the newcomers as pirates. This cruel advice had some semblence of justice, as the Dutch ship had some guns and ammunition but scarcely any merchandise on board. Ieyasu not only did not comply with the request of the Portuguese but treated the unfortunate survivors with kindness and consideration. William Adams, who was not only a good pilot but a capable shipbuilder and mathematician as well, very soon succeeded in winning Ieyasu's favor. The missionaries, realizing the danger of the presence of this staunch Protestant near the real ruler of Japan, tried by every possible means to neutralize his influence. They offered him their help in obtaining Ieyasu's

149

permission for his return to England, but he declined. They tried to convert him to Catholicism and failed.

Ieyasu, who for years had omitted nothing to attract as many foreign ships as possible to the ports of his Kantô domain, and who with regard to the Macao and Manila trade had even granted certain privileges to the missionaries, greatly rejoiced at having found an efficacious means of breaking the trade monopoly of the Iberians. Hence when Adams suggested to him that he enter into commercial relations with the Dutch he gladly agreed and dispatched the captain of the *De Liefde* to the Dutch fleet, which was crossing the South Sea. Not only did Dutch ships visit Japanese ports, but, what was even worse for the Portuguese, Dutch corsairs crippled the Macao trade by capturing many ships bound for Japan. The Portuguese, angry at the piracy and troublesome competition of the Dutch, complained to Ieyasu and asked him to exclude their rivals from Japan, since they were rebels to their king and by their piracy harming Japan. Adams and the Dutch paid them back in the same coin by telling Ieyasu that the Spaniards and Portuguese were robbers of foreign countries and aimed at nothing less than the conquest of Japan by means of the Christian missions. It is easy to see that Ieyasu's suspicions of the missionaries were reaffirmed since such charges seemed to confirm what in 1596 the ill-advised pilot of the *San Felipe* had said about Christian propaganda.

One of the reasons why Ieyasu did not start a general persecution soon after his rise to power was his fear of the opposition of the Christian *daimyô*. In 1601 he revoked his order against the Christian lords, Arima Harunobu and Ômura Yoshisaki, because they showed great firmness and were ready to die for their convictions. Among Ieyasu's partisans in the civil war of 1600 the Kurodas had distinguished themselves by their ardent zeal for the Tokugawa cause, and since Kuroda Yoshitaka had assumed the role of protector of the Christians, Ieyasu could not very well persecute them so long as Yoshitaka lived. Unfortunately for the Church he died in 1604, and his son, Nagamasa, although nominally a Christian, was by no means disposed or willing to take his father's place as protector of the Church. Perhaps the severest blow for the mission was the apostacy of Ômura Yoshisaki two years after Kuroda Yoshitaka's death. This seems to have been due to his suspicion that the Jesuits had a hand in his loss of the suburbs of Nagasaki, although in this he was entirely mistaken. In any event he called in the bonzes, expelled the Jesuits, and himself turned pagan. The apostacy of many

Christians was the inevitable result.

Thus one of the two princes who for nineteen years had been considered the pillars of the Church, one who had made the greatest sacrifices on her behalf, even to exposing his very life, had abandoned the faith and become a scandal to his brethren. Ieyasu, seeing himself freed of one of his chief opponents, spared no efforts in drawing Arima Harunobu to his side. Unfortunately, he succeeded although only after the lapse of a number of years.

In 1608 a band of Japanese, among them a number of Arima's retainers, had misbehaved at Macao and had been severely dealt with by the Captain General, André Pessoa. The rioters had challenged the authorities and offered armed resistance but, in the end, capitulated on condition their lives be spared. Pessoa, who after the lapse of his term as head of the colony of Macao intended to conduct the annual trade ship to Japan, feared that the survivors might spread one-sided reports on the incident after their return to Japan. He made them sign a document to the effect that they alone were to blame for what had happened and that they had been dealt with in strict justice. When, in 1609, Pessoa landed at Nagasaki he found himself in a most difficult situation. Hasegawa Sahyôe, governor of Nagasaki, would not allow him to sell his merchandise; the one-sided reports he received from the survivors of the Macao incident gave him a formidable weapon with which to destroy Pessoa. Moreover, two Dutch ships had arrived at Hirado and were waiting for a chance to capture Pessoa's ship, which had escaped them on its way to Japan. Arima Harunobu was greatly angered at the fate his people had met in the Macao incident and determined to avenge himself.

Ieyasu at first hesitated dealing severely with Pessoa, but the presence of the Dutch ships and the offer of the ex-governor of the Philippines, Rodrigo de Vivero, who happened at that time to be in Japan, to supply more goods than the Portuguese were able to export to Japan at last determined him to destroy Pessoa, even if consequentially no more Macao ships arrived. Arima was ordered to capture Pessoa and his ship, or to destroy him, if he should refuse to surrender or defended himself. After a three days fight Pessoa, not seeing any possibility of escape, blew up his ship and sank with it into Nagasaki harbor.

Arima, being the hero of the day, rose high in Ieyasu's favor. To attach him even more closely to his house, the latter offered the hand of one of his many granddaughters to Arima's eldest son, Naozumi. Although the latter was already married to an adopted daughter of the late Konishi Yukinaga, the offer of a close alliance with the ruling family was so enticing that Harunobu accepted it. If he had already created much scandal by his revengeful action against Pessoa, now the repudiation of the legitimate marriage of his son with a Christian lady was almost the equivalent of open apostacy. Thus the last pillar of the Church fell and, what is even more tragic, his unchristian behavior in another affair caused Ieyasu to begin his long-planned and long-expected war of extermination against the Church.

IX

The Great Persecution

Prelude

Arima Harunobu wanted to avail himself of Ieyasu's favor in advancing the interests of his family. The small fortress of Isahaya had formerly belonged to the Arima domain and so Harunobu resolved to recover it. To obtain his end the more speedily, he availed himself of the help of a Christian nobleman, Okamoto Daihachi, secretary to Ieyasu's powerful minister, Honda Masazumi. Although Arima spared neither words nor bribes, he made but little progress. When Harunobu finally grew impatient, Okamoto sent him a document to the effect that his petition had been granted. Since the document was but a cheap forgery, Okamoto soon after wrote that all had been spoiled by the intrigues of Arima's enemies, particularly Hasegawa Sahyôe, governor of Nagasaki. Seeing his cherished hopes frustated, Harunobu resolved to go himself to Ieyasu's court at Shizuoka and take the matter in his own hands. His eldest son Naozumi, who had been long waiting for his father's retirement from the daimyate, encouraged the latter in his resolution and even offered to accompany him to court, supposedly to help his father, but in reality to destroy him by disclosing to Ieyasu his dealings with Okamoto. In this he was encouraged by his new wife and by Hasegawa, his father's deadly enemy.

When Ieyasu learned what had happened, he condemned Okamoto to death, deposed and exiled Harunobu to the province of Kai. Struck by misfortune, the latter at last recognized his mistakes: his unchristian behavior towards Pessoa; the scandal he had raised by consenting to the unlawful marriage of his son; and, last, his intrigues in the Isahaya affair. He saw in his misfortune a just punishment of heaven. Simultaneouly he wrote to various friends by whose help he hoped to recover his fief. Naozumi thereupon denounced his father to Ieyasu, who condemned Harunobu to death. He received the sentence with truly Christian resignation and prepared himself for death by an act of contrition. As a *samurai* he had been granted the "privilege" of disemboweling himself rather than suffer the disgrace of execution, but as a Christian Harunobu refused to kill himself and asked one of his favored retainers to decapitate him.

Arima Naozumi had been granted the succession to his father's estate upon condition that he apostatize and lead his subjects back to paganism. When he returned from Shizuoka he expelled the missionaries, called in the bonzes and urged his principal retainers to apostatize, but met with a strong refusal. Thereupon a number of Christians were driven from their homes and deprived of all means of subsistence, but their heroism only strengthened the courage of their brethren. Even when Naozumi killed some of the most courageous, he could not shake the constancy of the rest. Despairing of final victory, he eventually asked Ieyasu to be changed to another fief and was given a much smaller domain in the province of Hyûga.

Ieyasu, who for years had concealed his hatred of Christianity, was greatly scandalized by Arima Harunobu's and Naozumi's unchristian behavior and ordered all Christians in his service to give up their faith. The fourteen out of eighteen who refused to obey were deprived of their goods, dismissed from service and exiled to Tsugaru, the Aomori prefecture of today. Even Christian ladies were not spared. The most courageous of them, the Korean court lady Julia, was exiled to the island of Ôshima in Tôkyô Bay. It has been stated above that of all churches in Japan only those of Nagasaki, Ôsaka, Edo and lower Kyôto as well as the churches of Arima and Ômura were legally recognized and that all the rest could be suppressed at any time without any new legal enactment. The Franciscan church at Kyôto and the Jesuit church at upper-Kyôto were now suppressed.

Ieyasu's example was followed by a number of *daimyô*. At Higo persecution flared up once more; at Bungo the missionaries were exiled from Takata and Notsu; and in Chikuzen the Christian *samurai* were called upon to apostatize. Hosokawa Tadaoki, who since the tragic death of his Christian wife, Gracia, had been one of the warmest friends of the Fathers, yielded to moral pressure and in 1611 expelled the missionaries from his capital of Kokura. Fukushmia Masanori of Hiroshima, however, continued to favor the Church as did Maeda Toshinaga of Kanazawa, Takayama Ukon's suzerain. Both of them responded to Ieyasu's pressure only in so far as they heeded his strict prohibition against giving help or shelter to those Christians he had exiled to Tsugaru.

During the year 1613 a violent persecution raged in Arima and in the city of Edo, where Ieyasu's son, Hidetada, beheaded twenty-eight Christians, for the most part lepers. In the rest of the country conditions had become again more or less normal, so that it seemed as if the danger had passed. Yet it was only the quiet immediately before the storm. Only a trifling incident was needed to arouse violent fury. One occurred towards the end of the same year.

The Edict of Exile

One of the fiercest enemies of Christianity was Hasegawa Sahyôe, the governor of Nagasaki. Towards the end of 1613 he proceeded to Ieyasu's court, firmly resolved to induce the latter to exterminate the foreign religion. He told the ruler that in Arima the Christians had venerated the martyrs executed as rebels against the laws of the land and had taken relics of their dead bodies home as objects of worship. He furthermore reported that the Christians of Nagasaki had adored a criminal at the very moment when the executioner gave him the deathblow. This is what had happened: a Christian had sold unstamped silver bars and thus forfeited his life. He was condemned to die on the cross and to be executed with five others, who were to be decapitated. When the executioner was about to pierce the heart of the Christian with a lance, his Christian brethren knelt down to offer prayers to the Lord in his behalf. This act of Christian charity was interpreted as "adoration of a criminal" by the pagans and as such reported to Hasegawa and through him to Ieyasu, who was aroused to such a fit of anger that he exclaimed: "A law which teaches such things is from the devil." At once he charged Hasegawa to expel all missionaries from Japan and simultaneously urged all the *daimyô* to spare no efforts to make the Christians apostatize.

On January 27, 1614, Ieyasu issued a lengthy decree which marks the beginning of the most violent, cruel and systematic of persecutions. It represented Christianity as a danger to the national religions, the independence of the country and the moral order and threatened to exterminate it completely. All missionaries were strictly ordered to leave the country and the Christians to return to the religion of their ancestors. The author of the document was the Neo-Confucianist Hayashi Razan, who in it professes himself an orthodox Confucianist, but at the same time points out the principal doctrines of Buddhism and *Shintô* and finally declares Christianity a menace to all three religions of the country.

The edict was officially made known to the missionaries in Kyôto on February 14, together with orders to leave the city within five days and to proceed to Nagasaki to be deported. Since Ieyasu meant what he said, it was impossible for the missionaries to disregard his order, and so the great majority of them left for Nagasaki. Only very few remained hidden in various parts of the country.

Not only the missionaries but also the leading Christians were affected by Ieyasu's decree. Shortly after the decree's publication, Maeda Toshinaga, *daimyô* of the three provinces of Kaga, Noto and Etchû, received orders to deport Takayama Ukon and Naitô Tadatoshi with their families to Kyôto if they should refuse to give up their faith. For these valiant champions of Christ it was a matter of course to choose exile and even death rather than apostatize, and so they submitted cheerfully to the unjust order. Itakura Katsushige, governor of Kyôto, being afraid that the presence of such fearless men as Takayama and Naitô would enhance the courage of the Christians, did not allow them to enter the capital but told them to wait at Sakamoto until he should receive definite instructions from Ieyasu. After the lapse of 30 days came Ieyasu's answer: The men were to be deported to Nagasaki, but the women were to be set at liberty. The latter chose, however, to share the fate of their husbands, fathers and brothers and went with them to Nagasaki.

Even before the publication of the edict of exile the governor of Kyôto had received orders to draw up a list of the Christians in the capital. Since it turned out to contain 4,000 names, Itakura, fear-

ing Ieyasu's anger at such an enormous figure, took
a new census in which the names of children and
servants were to be omitted. When he presented
this new list of 1,600 Christians to Ieyasu, he was
greatly rebuked for his negligence in not having
prevented the spread of the foreign religion. Had
Ieyasu known that the actual number of Christians
was no less than 7,000, his fury would probably
have known no bounds.

Ieyasu thought that it would not be too difficult
to make the Christians of the capital apostatize by
means of threats and promises, but since he knew
that the kindhearted governor, who was a friend
of the Christians, would be loath to adopt severe
methods, he called upon Ôkubo Tadachika, *daimyô*
of Odawara, to undertake the unpleasant task. This
was a very clever trick, for Tadachika was under
the suspicion of being involved in a purported plot
of the late Ôkubo Nagayasu, Ieyasu's minister of
finance, and so he would very likely display extraordinary zeal to appease his lord and clear himself
of all suspicion. Towards the end of February,
1614, Tadachika appeared in Kyôto with 300 armed
men, tore down the churches, burnt the debris outside the city and threatened to deliver all Christians to death at the stake, if they would not immediately return to the religion of their forefathers.
Since his threats made no impression on the Chris-

tians, Tadachika urged their relatives, friends and
neighbors to leave nothing untried to make them
give up their faith, but the majority of them remained firm. Thereupon Tadachika announced
that he would put the recalcitrants into rice bags,
have them carried in disgrace through the streets
and burnt at the stake, but even this made no impression upon the Christians. At last Tadachika
resolved to carry out his threats and chose as his
first victims the Christian women who lived near
the Jesuit church in a quasi-monastery under the
direction of the heroic Julia Naitô, sister of Naitô
Tadatoshi. If they were to refuse to give up their
faith, they would be stripped naked and led through
the streets of the city. Julia hid the nine youngest
of her companions in the houses of friends, but
she with the other nine prepared for the ordeal.

On the appointed day they were tied hand and
foot, put into rice bags and carried two by two,
dangling on sticks, through the streets of Kyôto.
Outside the city they were thrown down on the
snowy ground and remained for the rest of the day
exposed to the cold. The bonzes urged them to
say simply that they were no longer Christians,
but all remained firm. In similar fashion the Christians of Kyôto and Ôsaka, men, women and even
children, were tortured without any tangible results. Since Ieyasu had not given Tadachika per-

mission to shed blood, he could do no more than throw his victims in jail and ask for further instructions. Ieyasu finally gave orders to deport the recalcitrant Christians to Tsugaru and Julia Naitô with her companions to Nagasaki whence they would be exiled to Macao and Manila. Yet before this order reached Kyôto, Tadachika fell into disgrace, was exiled and his castle seized by Ieyasu. All his zeal against the poor Christians did not save him from the impending blow, and the clever Ieyasu availed himself of his absence to take possession of Odawara Castle without sacrificing a single life.

The Missionaries Exiled

At Nagasaki the assembled missionaries were waiting for months for their deportation, but at the same time hoped against hope that Ieyasu would either revoke his decree or at least allow some Fathers to remain at Nagasaki to take care of the Portuguese merchants. That Ieyasu did not at once expel the missionaries from the country was probably because he was afraid that the Macao ships would thereby cease to call at his ports. It was rumored that both he and Hasegawa were anxiously waiting for the arrival of a ship and time and again expressed fear and doubts whether it would come at all.

The Great Persecution

Seeing themselves destitute of all human help, the Christians and missionaries implored heaven to avert the impending disaster. Great processions were held from Ascension Day until the feast of *Corpus Christi,* that is for three weeks, to obtain from the Lord the revocation of the edict. The pagans suspected these demonstrations and it was announced to Ieyasu that they were clear signs of a planned rebellion. The expeditionary force which was sent to crush this "rebellion" easily found out that nothing was to be feared of these purely religious processions.

When finally in June the Macao ship dropped anchor at Nagasaki, Ieyasu and Hasegawa greatly rejoiced that their fear had been groundless. This again gave new hope to the Fathers of averting the fatal blow, and they urged the captain to send an embassy to Ieyasu with a rich present so as to appease his wrath. The embassy was received very courteously, but when it presented its request in behalf of the missionaries, Ieyasu grew angry and flatly refused to consider the proposition. Before this sad news reached Nagasaki, Hasegawa had been ordered to make the last preparations for the deportation of the missionaries. On October 27, they were told to leave Nagasaki and to live in straw huts on the shore until the departure of the vessels. Simultaneously all churches which had

not as yet been destroyed were torn down and
their materials burnt. The Macao ship, not as yet
having disposed of its merchandise, was supposed
to remain for several months longer in Nagasaki
harbor, but since Ieyasu insisted upon the immediate deportation of the missionaries the only vessels available were a number of miserable junks.
On November 7 and 8 the missionaries, Julia
Naitô and her sisters as well as a number of promi-
nent Japanese Christians had to board these junks,
two of which were bound for Manila and three for
Macao and Siam. Of the Jesuits sixty-two, among
them thirty-three priests, went to Macao; eight
priests, fifteen Japanese brothers and fifteen catechists (*dôjiku*) to Manila; whereas eighteen priests
and nine brothers remained in Japan. The Jesuit
Provincial Valentin Carvalho went on board a junk
bound for Macao but hoped to disembark on some
deserted island and to return to Japan. This proved
impossible. Some of the friars and five of the
seven Japanese secular priests, however, managed
to return in this way to their deserted flocks. At
least thirty-seven priests remained in the country:
five secular priests, seven Dominicans, six Franciscans, one Augustinian and eighteen Jesuits. In
vain the Jesuits had asked that Father Mesquita,
who was at the point of death, be allowed to remain
until the departure of the Macao ship. He had

to leave Nagasaki but died before the junks set sail.

Among the exiles bound for Manila were the two heroic figures, Takayama Ukon and Naitô Tadatoshi, with their families. At Manila they were given a hearty welcome, but shortly after their arrival Takayama was seized with a deadly fever and died on February 4, 1615. He was buried in the Jesuit church, because it was hoped that some day he would be raised to the honor of the altars, which, however, has not yet happened.

Martyrdoms

Ieyasu did not shed Christian blood, probably because he believed that without pastors Christianity was doomed, even if it might take a number of years to die. It must, moreover, be admitted, in all justice, that he did not like to kill his adversaries unless it seemed to be the only effective means of meeting possible dangers on their part, and the Jesuit letters time and again pay tribute to his humane character. Ieyasu, already very old, did not wish to be branded a tyrant for acts of terror during his last years and, moreover, he knew that his successors would take sterner measures against the Christians, if need should arise. The fact that he began his war of extermination just then and there may be explained by his desire to eliminate possible danger on the part of Christian *daimyô* and *samurai* in his inevitable struggle with Hideyori, whom he had pushed aside.

The war with the son of the late Hideyoshi started almost immediately after the deportation of the missionaries and the leading Christian *samurai* and lasted, with a short interruption, until the summer of 1615. As a matter of fact, not a few Christian *samurai* fought on Hideyori's side and thereby added new fuel to Ieyasu's hostility towards the foreign religion. Yet at the same time the Ôsaka struggle gave the Christians some respite, since the attention of the whole country was centered on the outcome of the duel between the two great houses, each of which claimed the right to rule Japan. The war ended with the annihilation of Hideyori and the triumph of the Tokugawa, whose grip on Japan was thereby assured for many generations to come.

Apart from the persecution in Arima, where since 1612 many had been killed by the apostate *daimyô,* there were few martyrs in the rest of Japan until the end of the Ôsaka struggle, and even during the following year their number was comparatively small. The situation changed completely, however, with Ieyasu's death, which occurred in the early days of 1616. His son Hidetada had killed many Christians in his capital of Edo in 1613, and it was to be expected that the persecution would grow in violence when he would no longer be restrained by the more humane policy of his father. When it became known that a number of missionaries had remained in the country, they were hunted like wild beasts, and on April 29, 1617, two of them were decapitated at Ômura. In the following year a great many martyrs died in various parts of the country, particularly in Kyûshû. One of the most violent persecutors was Hosokawa Tadaoki, who for many years had been the friend of protector of the Christians. Even a number of formerly Christian *daimyô* like Kuroda Nagamasa of Chikuzen, Matsura Takanobu of Hirado, and Ômura Yoshisaki of Ômura became violent persecutors. The fury of persecution went on unabated during the year 1619. In 1620 and 1621 only a few Christians suffered martyrdom, although a great many awaited death in the jails of Nagasaki and Ômura.

In 1622 occurred the "great martyrdom" of Nagasaki, where twenty-three Christians, among them a good many missionaries, were burnt at the stake and twenty-two, for the most part hosts of the priests with their wives and children, beheaded. This great holocaust was the last act of Hidetada's cruelty, for on January 31, 1623, he retired from the office of *shôgun* in favor of his son,

Iemitsu, the third Tokugawa *shôgun*.

If the Christians had expected a relaxation of the persecution on the part of the new *shôgun,* they were most cruelly disappointed, for Iemitsu greatly surpassed his father in cruelty and was, in fact, the most violent persectuor of all Tokugawa *shôguns.* Until then most of the martyrdoms had occurred in Kyûshû, but now persecution spread to all parts of the country, particularly to Edo and the northeast. On December 4, 1623, fifty victims died in the flames under the very eyes of the tyrant Iemitsu in Edo and twenty-four more in the same month. In the following year persecution spread to the northeastern provinces, where until then there had been comparative quiet. As a result, many Christians from Kyûshû and southwestern Japan had sought refuge in these districts. Mass martyrdoms occurred in 1624 in Edo, Kubota, near Akita, and Dewa, and a number of them also in Sendai, where for a number of years the mighty Date Masamune had closed his eyes to the presence of many Christians.

The poor Christians of Arima had enjoyed comparative peace for more than ten years under the mild rule of Matsukura Shigemasa, Arima Naozumi's successor. When, however, several foreign missionaries had been discovered in his domain, he was greatly reprimanded by Iemitsu and, in order to win back the *shôgun's* favor, started a most violent and cruel persecution in 1627. Many Christians were decapitated, burnt at the stake, and, above all, tortured and killed in the hot sulphurous springs of Mount Unzen. Under his son, Shigeharu, occurred the famous Shimabara insurrection with the complete annihilation of the once so flourishing Christian community of Arima. Simultaneous with the recrudescence of the persecution in Arima hundreds of Christians were massacred in all parts of the country, particularly in Nagasaki, Ômura and the northeastern provinces.

It would be tedious to enumerate all the acts of violence and brutality committed against the harassed Christians and their pastors, but the few instances related may give a general idea of the fury of this most terrible persecution. The persecutors were well aware that entire districts would be depopulated, if all Christians were to be killed, and thus from the very beginning they were anxious to make apostates rather than martyrs.

This accounts for the fact that as time went on the martyrdoms became more and more cruel. Ordinary death penalties by decapitation or crucifixion did not shake the constancy of the Christians. Consequently the victims were burned at the stake and, in order that their agony might be prolonged, the wood was placed at some distance and the sufferers roasted by the slow fire. When even this terrible torture proved insufficient, Iemitsu invented the martyrdom of the pit, the torture of *tsurushi,* to which even the most courageous succumbed. The victim's body and extremities were tightly tied with rope. His feet were fastened to a rack and his body was lowered head first into a ditch up to the waist.

To prevent a rapid death as the result of circulatory obstruction, the torturers would bleed the victim at the temples and so prolong his agony. In this way the torment could be made to last several days, sometimes even an entire week, until death made an end to this intolerable torture. As a result the number of apostacies grew since only the most valiant of heroes could endure the unspeakable agony.

The final tragedy of the peak of Iemitsu's persecution was the Shimabara insurrection (1637–1638). Its outbreak was not due, as is often maintained, to violent persecutions by Matsukura Shigeharu, but to his intolerable fiscal exploitation of the poor peasants of Arima. The last penny was extorted from them by the most violent acts of cruelty. On one occasion a peasant fled to the mountains when the tax collector was expected. The latter seized his daughter, stripped her naked and burnt her entire body with flaming torches.

Learning of this barbarous act of violence, the father of the girl with a number of friends attacked the residence of the tax collector and slew everybody they came across. This happened on December 17, 1637, and was the signal for the general insurrection of the peasants of Arima. They were reinforced by the malcontents of Amakusa, who came over from the Archipelago.

The *shôgun* dispatched an army of 30,000 warriors, but it could not reduce the peasants' stronghold of Harajô and suffered heavy casualties. Its general, Itakura Shigemasa, was killed in battle. At last a large army of about 100,000 men arrived from various parts of the country, and finally the fortress was taken. Among the insurgents were not only Christians but a good number of pagans. The latter had been promised forgiveness if they would come over and, as a matter of fact, they made use of this offer. The Christians, however, being threatened with death unless they would apostatize, preferred to die rather than give up their faith. Thus the insurrection in the end became a religious war. The castle was stormed on April 15, 1638. All fighting men were killed in battle or after surrender, but the women and children were offered their lives if they would apostatize. All of them preferred to die rather than become traitors to their faith and were presently decapitated. The number of victims of the Shimabara holocaust is estimated at between 35,000 and 37,000 souls. Not a single Christian was left in Arima, which until 1612 had been an entirely Christian country.

Japan Closed to Foreign Intercourse

In spite of the most cruel persecutions and the ever growing number of apostacies, the *shôgun's* government nevertheless thought it necessary to resort to various other extreme methods to exterminate Christianity more quickly and more surely. As early as 1627 the ceremony of *efumi* or picture treading was introduced. Those suspected of being Christians had to appear before the magistrate and were called upon to tread on a picture of Christ or His Holy Mother. If they complied with this order, they were considered apostates; if they refused, they had to die. *Efumi* was confined to the areas which had been more or less entirely Christian, but as Christians fled to various parts of the country, another device was invented, by which any Christian in any part of Japan might easily be discovered, the so-called *shûmon aratame,* literally: examination of religion. It required that every Japanese appear once a year in a temple or before a magistrate, declare officially to which Buddhist sect he belonged and sign his declaration for himself and all the members of his family. Thus no Christian could remain unknown, unless he at least outwardly professed a Buddhist sect. The earliest extant records of *shûmon aratame,* which started in 1623, go back to the year 1635, whereas the latest are dated 1871.

At all times it has proved very effective to tyrannical governments to enlist avarice in their efforts to destroy their enemies, by putting a price on their heads. As early as 1634 the *shôgun's* government promised a high reward to anyone informing against a priest, brother, catechist or Christian. These prices were raised several times until in 1682 they amounted to the following sums: 500 *ryô* or silver pieces for the informer of a priest; 300 *ryô* for the informer of a brother; the same amount for the informer of a converted apostate; 100 *ryô* for the informer of a person who gave shelter to a Christian or a catechumen; he who gave information on a house actually offering hospitality to a Christian might receive up to 500 *ryô* according to the importance of the respective house. As early as 1634 it was strictly forbidden for Japanese to go abroad, lest they become Christians or even priests and return to Japan to propagate Christianity.

It will be recalled that in 1614 the rulers of Japan feared that the Macao ships might no longer call at Japanese ports if Christianity were to be outlawed and the missionaries expelled. This fear proved not only altogether unfounded, but the government of Macao gave strict orders that no missionary should smuggle himself into Japan on a Macao ship. The Japan trade was a life and death question for the city of Macao, and so the interests of religion had to be sacrificed, for only in this way could the lucrative trade be safeguarded.

The Macao ships came to Japan as before and did good business, although many a craft was seized by the Dutch on its way to Japan and the former trade monopoly had long ago been destroyed by Dutch competition. In 1623 the English had voluntarily withdrawn from Japan and in the following year the Spaniards were expelled, but the Portuguese ships were unmolested until 1635. When in that year the Macao craft arrived in Japan, it had to drop anchor at the artificial island of Deshima, which had been built expressly for this purpose. The Portuguese merchants were watched closely and treated little better than prisoners, and in the following year Portuguese ships were altogether excluded from Japan. The Shimabara insurrection still further increased the suspicion of the government, since it wrongly believed that the rebellion had been fomented and aided by Christian powers from abroad. As a result, the

Dutch factory was moved from Hirado to Deshima, where the Dutch could trade and be closely watched. Apart from the Dutch ship and Chinese junks no foreign vessel was henceforth to land in Japan, and the coast was heavily guarded so as to enforce this prohibition. Thus for more than 200 years, from 1638 to 1854, Japan was practically cut off from the rest of the world.

The Number of Christians and Martrys

There has been a good deal of pious exaggeration concerning the numbers of Christians from 1549 to 1614 and those who su ered martyrdom for their faith. The figures given by the Jesuit missionaries for the years 1571 (30,000), 1579 (100,000), 1582 (150,000), 1587 (200,000) would seem to correspond to actual facts. Father Frois, asserting that in 1597 there were about 300,000 Christians in Japan, probably exaggerates, for although we are told time and again that from 1599 to 1600 at least 70,000 converts were made, according to Bishop Cerqueira there were no more than 300,000 Christians in 1600. From 1600 to 1612 the Church enjoyed comparative peace and every year from 5,000 to 7,000 converts were made, yet in 1614 the number of Christians was at the most 300,000 and probably less. In other words, from 1600 on there was no actual increase, and if every year several thousands were baptized, a more or less equal number must have fallen away, which is explicitly stated by such weighty historians as Bartoli and Trigault. There were a good many baptisms after 1614, but the great number of apostacies during the most violent persecution undoubtedly by far exceeded the number of neophytes.

The number of martyrs has been exaggerated even more than that of converts. The Japanese scholar and statesman Arai Hakuseki estimates the victims of the persecution until 1651 at 200,000 or 300,000. He undoubtedly includes all who suffered in any way for the sake of their faith, and in this sense he is correct, for all Christians were subjected to great hardships, even if they were not killed. For those who actually gave their life for Christ, we have to discount, however, such astronomical figures. Father Cardim lists in his catalogue of martyrs (Rome, 1646) about 1,450 victims and gives a great many names. Pagès, Delplace and Anesaki give much larger figures, which very recently have again been increased by the studies of Father Marega, so that at present we know of no less than 4,045 well documented martyrdoms. Of these 3,171 shed their blood for Christ and 874 died in jail or as a result of starvation, misery and similar causes. Considering that there were in 1614 at the most 300,000 Christians in Japan, over

4,000 martyrs is indeed a very high percentage. If the victims of the Shimabara insurrection, who are not considered martyrs, although they died for being Christians, are included, more than thirteen percent of all Christians lost their lives for the sake of their faith. This is probably unequalled in the annals of the Church.

X

Christianity During the Seclusion

Persecution Unabated

Having killed practically all missionaries, compelled numberless Christians to apostatize and sealed the frontiers against any possible help from Christian countries, the shôgunal government believed itself not yet sufficiently protected against the detested foreign religion. Although all, who were suspected of being Christians, were compelled by *efumi* to declare themselves clearly and, moreover, every Japanese had every year to state his religious affiliation, it was, nevertheless, thought necessary to search positively and systematically for Christians. For this reason high rewards had been promised in 1634 and were subsequently twice increased so as to yield the greatest possible results. Over and above all, in 1640 an inquisition tribunal was established in the mansion of the apostate

181

The Catholic Church in Japan

Inouye Seibei, at Koishikawa in Edo. A host of
spies and numerous hunters of Christians were
mobilized to search for adherents of the proscribed
religion throughout the country and to deliver
them to the great inquisitor. The torture of the
pit, which since 1633 had proved so effective for
making apostates, in nearly all cases had the desired effect.

Since the beginning of the great persecution it
had from year to year become more difficult to
smuggle missionaries into Japan from abroad, until
finally the city of Macao strictly prohibited any
priest to go on board a ship bound for Japan, since
otherwise the city would lose what little was left
of the indispensible Japan trade. This prohibition
became, however, obsolete when in 1636 Portuguese ships were no longer admitted to Japanese
ports. Since the Spaniards had been excluded
twelve years earlier, missionaries could venture to
reach Japan through the Philippines without having to fear opposition on the part of the governor
of Manila. As a result, many attempts were made
to enter Japan in this way, and although most of
them failed, some at least met with success. On
August 11, 1642, Father Rubino, S.J., landed with
four Jesuit priests and three laymen on an island
of Satsuma, but very soon they were seized and
carried to Nagasaki, where they arrived on August

21. They were exposed to the most terrible tortures and finally condemned to the pit. They were martyred in March, 1643.

During the same year another group of missionaries, four Jesuit priests, one brother and five laymen, among them three Japanese Christians, landed at the island of Ôshima, in the province of Chikuzen. They were immediately arrested, taken to Edo and subjected to the torture of the pit. It seems that they grew weak and at least outwardly apostatized. Only one of the priests revoked his apostacy and died soon after in jail; the others were certainly not martyred but were also not let free, as might be expected had they actually apostatized. They lived under strict supervision in the compound of the inquisition, the *Kirishitan Yashiki,* and died a natural death. One of them, Father Joseph Chiara, lived to a very old age and died only in 1685. The apparent failure of these men, who had come all the way from the most distant parts of the world to devote their lives to the bereaved Christians of Japan, is an eloquent proof of the awfulness of the torture of the pit and its efficacy in making apostates, for which it had been invented.

Although the number of martyrs had dwindled and that of apostates soared since the application of the martyrdom of the pit, there occurred quite a number of holocausts even after the closing of the country. In 1649, twenty-three Christians died in the pit at Nagasaki, and in the following year seventy-four, among them women and children, were decapitated in the same city. In 1658, at Nagasaki, Ômura, Saga, Hirado and Shimabara of 608 Christians incarcerated 411 were killed, 78 died in prison, 20 were punished by lifelong imprisonment and only 99 released. In Bungo from 1660 to 1691 no less than 510 Christians were prosecuted. Of these 486 were killed or died in prison before 1691 and 24 were still living in jail. In 1665 many Christian communities in northern Owari were banished from home and detained in segregated settlements; in 1667 in Mino and Owari about 2,000 Christians were arrested and many killed. The last great martyrdom known occurred in 1697 in the province of Mino with no less than 35 victims. All of these mass martyrdoms and many lesser ones have become known only during the last thirty years, and others are coming to light almost every year. Thus it appears that even when the Japanese Christians were deprived of all spiritual help of their priests they were ready to lay down their lives for their faith, a splendid vindication of Saint Francis Xavier's assertion that the Japanese Christians were ready to make any sacrifice, once they had recognized the truth of the Christian religion.

184

Christianity During the Seclusion

Father Sidotti

The heroism of the martyr Church of Japan during the period of seclusion was made known abroad occasionally through Dutch or Chinese merchants and inspired many apostolic men to risk their lives so as to bring help to these abandoned heroes. One of them at least, Father John Baptist Sidotti, succeeded in landing on the island of Yakushima, in the province of Ôsumi, in 1708. The Spanish vessel which had brought him to Japan left him on the deserted shore and immediately returned to Manila. At once the courageous priest was arrested and brought to Edo for trial. No less a person than the famous philosopher and statesman Arai Hakuseki examined him. Arai asked Sidotti many things about the West and subsequently published an account of it under the title *Seiyô Kibun* (An Account of the West). Although he was by no means a friend of the Christian religion, he, nevertheless, did not share the popular prejudice that it threatened the political independence of Japan. He had the greatest respect and admiration for the intrepid and heroic priest, who had come all the way from Italy to a life of hardship and at the risk of his life for the salvation of his brethren in religion. Thus Arai proposed to send Sidotti back to the Philippines, but his advice was not heeded. Yet Sidotti's life

The Catholic Church in Japan

was spared, nor was he, it would seem, even subjected to any kind of torture. He was interned in the *Kirishitan Yashiki* and treated humanely for about seven years, but when he endeavored to make converts and baptized his guard, he was thrown into a dark cell and died shortly after from starvation an dexhaustion on November 16, 1715.

Vain Attempts by the City of Macao

The Japan trade had been for nearly one hundred years the main source of income for the city of Macao, and so it is easy to see that its loss was a most fatal blow to the tiny colony. As a result, it left nothing untried to recover this loss and restore commercial intercourse with the insular empire. Despite the strictest prohibition and the most terrible punishment which awaited the transgressor, the city in 1640 sent an embassy to Nagasaki with rich presents and a proposal for the restoration of the Macao-Japan trade. They not only failed in their attempt, but their ship was seized at once, and the ambassadors together with entire crew, sixty-one in all, were thrown in jail. Refusing to apostatize, they were decapitated and their heads exposed. Their ship was burned.

Only thirteen colored mariners were spared and sent back on a miserable junk to report to the city of Macao what had happened to its ship and embassy. This was the message they brought from Japan: "So long as the sun warms the earth, let no Christian be so bold as to come to Japan, and let all know that if King Philip himself, or even the very God of the Christians, or the great Buddha contravene this prohibition, they shall pay for it with their heads."

In spite of the terrible fate meted out to its ambassadors, Macao soon made another attempt to restore commercial intercourse with Japan. On December 13, 1640, Portugal had succeeded in shaking off the yoke of the Spanish rulers and raised John of Braganza to the Portuguese throne. The severance of Portugal from Spanish rule seemed to the citizens of Macao a ray of hope for the restoration of the Japan trade.

They believed that the shôgunate had banned their ships from Japan solely because of their political ties with Spain, which threatened, so they believed, national independence. Hence the new king of Portugal, John IV, was asked to send an ambassador to Japan and propose resumption of the trade with Macao. The ambassador, Don Gonzalo de Siqueira, arrived at Nagasaki on July 16, 1647. He refused to surrender his ammunition and the rudders of his ship and was subsequently blockaded by a force of 50,000 men. Even so he remained adamant to the request of the Japanese, who had meanwhile informed the *shôgun* of his arrival and asked for proper instructions. On August 28, the *shôgun's* minister and the governor of Nagasaki presented to Siqueira a letter from Edo, according to which he was allowed to leave the harbor unmolested, but his request for the reopening of commercial relations was flatly refused.

A third attempt was made in 1685. The Jesuit priest Anthony Thomas had been planning since 1679 the resumption of the Japanese mission with the financial assistance of the Duchess Maria d'Aveiro. He prevailed upon the Viceroy of India to send an embassy to Japan and prepared its dispatch at Macao. Meanwhile a small Japanese craft was shipwrecked in the Macao waters, and the twelve survivors were offered hospitality by the city. They told about the condition of Christianity in Japan, were instructed in the faith and baptized. The repatriation of these ship-wrecks afforded an unexpected opportunity to dispatch the embassy for which Father Thomas had been working for years. To his regret the good Father could not go to Japan, because he had just been requested by the Chinese Emperor Kang-hsi as assistant to Father Verbiest at the astronomical institute in Peking. The embassy actually embarked for Japan on June 1, 1585, and arrived at Nagasaki on July 3.

Christianity During the Seclusion

The Japanese authorities sent an interpreter with a number of others on board to inquire after their demand. The Portuguese asked for an interview with the *shôgun*. All their answers were carefully noted down as well as those of the twelve Japanese survivors. The Japanese treated the unwelcome guests courteously and considerately. Next day their luggage was carefully searched for holy pictures, rosaries, crosses and the like, and then they were allowed to land. All arms, ammunition, the rudders and the sails of the ship were taken by the Japanese with the assurance they would return them when the ship had been granted permission to return home. The matter was reported to Edo, and in the meantime the Portuguese were often visited by the interpreters and were well provided by the governor with victuals and water, but they were watched closely and not permitted to go on land.

On August 6, the reply of the *shôgun* came. The Portuguese were told they could return to Macao whenever they wished and were offered all they needed for their home journey. At the same time they were told to ask the governor of Macao never again to send ships to Japan, not because the twelve Japanese had there been instructed in the Christian religion, but because the law of the country strictly and under the heaviest penalties prohibited foreign ships from landing in Japan. Concerning the twelve Japanese survivors which privy counsellors reported sent to the prime minister of the *shôgun,* the *Nagasaki Kiroku* a manuscript Japanese journal, says that the twelve were sent home, having been interned at Nagasaki for some time, yet the journal does not say what happened to them after their return to their native place.

On the next day the governor of Nagasaki sent a lavish amount of food to the Portuguese, asked the captain to anchor at some distance from the harbor and wanted to know when he would set sail for Macao.

Because of unfavorable weather the departure of the ship was delayed for some time, but on September 23 it safely returned to Macao. Since this most promising venture had failed, Macao made no further attempt to penetrate into the closed insular empire. Yet a few years earlier the English had sent a ship to Nagasaki to resume their trade with Japan, which they had voluntarily abandoned as early as 1623. Their attempt failed on the plea that their king, Charles II, was married to a Portuguese princess. Japan remained closed until 1854 when the American Commodore Perry forced open the gates.

Christianity During the Seclusion

Faith Preserved

Since the introduction of *efumi* and of *shûmon aratame,* it was absolutely impossible for a Christian to hide his faith, and if for one reason or other a Christian could have remained unknown, the price put on his head or the spies and agents of the inquisition would surely sooner or later bring about his arrest and prosecution. As a result, the Christians in the end were led to the belief that they could lawfully comply with the request of the authorities, at least outwardly, if in their hearts they kept the faith, since this seemed the only possible way of transmitting Christianity to their children. Providence permitted this error and thus preserved the faith for more than 200 years despite the most awful persecution. Because of the total lack of priests and the extreme scarcity of books on Christian doctrine this would not have been possible had not peculiar circumstances favored the abandoned flock.

From the very beginning the Japanese mission had been suffering from an extreme shortage of priests and catechists. In 1559 there were no more than three priests in Japan to take care of the Christians of Bungo and its dependencies, of Yamaguchi and of Hirado. Only because of the expulsion from everywhere except Bungo was it possible to start a mission in Gokinai. In Kyôto and surroundings there was only one priest for more than four years although he had to take care of more than half a dozen churches and chapels. When in 1581 Valignano visited Takatsuki neither resident priest nor brother was there to minister to the enormous flock of 18,000 Christians. There had been mass baptisms in Ômura, Arima, Amakusa and Bungo from 1574 to 1581, but the shortage of missionaries made it impossible to instruct these numerous neophytes properly and many of them were Christians in name only.

Father Valignano was so deeply impressed by this desperate situation that he actually hesitated to push the work of evangelization. He, nevertheless, convinced himself that it was necessary to speed up the work. The training of native helpers was to solve the problem, but it required years before the seminaries could turn out large numbers of catechists, and the first native priests were ordained only in 1601. Their numbers were never considerable even in later years.

A comparison of the statistics of missionaries and Christians will show that this shortage of workers continued to handicap the mission all through the 80 years following Xavier's arrival. In 1580 there were in Japan 59 Jesuits and among them only 28 priests, who had to take care of about 130,000 Christians. During the following 10 years the number of Jesuits grew rapidly until it reached its peak in 1590 with 47 priests, 68 brothers and 25 novices, but in the meantime the number of Christians had risen to over 200,000. From then on the Jesuits decreased in numbers so that in 1614 they were 120 priests and brothers, the number of novices not being given in the printed sources. After 1602, friars from the Philippines shared in the work with the Jesuits, but their combined numbers, including seven secular priests, amounted to no more than 35 priests in 1614 against about 60 Jesuit Fathers. Thus shortly before the outbreak of the persecution 95 priests had to minister to about 300,000 Christians and simultaneously make from 5,000 to 7,000 new converts every year. This enormous task could not possibly be accomplished without the help of laymen.

We know that in 1584 the Jesuits employed 102 catechists or *dôjiku* and about 350 other lay helpers so that the entire missionary staff, including 84 Jesuits, was 500 persons. In 1603 it consisted of 126 Jesuits, 284 catechists, 170 church eldermen and other lay helpers, their sum total being 900. Apart from hired lay helpers many fervent Christians gratuitously worked for the preservation of the faith and spread of the Gospel. Many churches were only occasionally visited by a priest, and many Christians could not receive the sacraments for years, because no priest came to visit them. As a result, from the very beginning every Christian congregation had its regular organization of catechists, church elders, Sodalities of the Blessed Virgin and Brotherhoods, particularly the Misericordia, a charitable organization for helping the poor, visiting the sick, assisting the dying and burying the dead. It also happened at times that one single Christian founded a new congregation, where a missionary had never been before. Then he would ask for the visit of a priest to baptize the catechumens he had been instructing or, if no priest could obtained, he would take his would-be Christians to the next mission and have them baptized. In other words, the lay-apostolate played an unusually important part in the Japanese mission from the very beginning.

What had been a necessity even during times of peace, became the salvation of the Church during the long years of persecution. After the reopening of Japan lay organizations for the ministration of the faithful and mutual help for the preservation of the faith amidst the most awful trials were found by the missionaries wherever the faith had survived. This happened only in those cases where an entire village, town or large group of people were Christians. It is splendid proof that the policy of the early Jesuits in converting whole districts or provinces and creating a Christian atmosphere was sound and wise. Every Christian community had its catechist or *oshie-kata,* who taught prayers and Christian doctrine, and one or several baptizers or *mizu-kata,* who baptized the new-born children. Since baptism was administered in Latin, it was essential that the correct formula be faithful transmitted from generation to generation. For this reason every baptizer had a disciple, who, after an apprenticeship of at least five years, was to take over the office of his master, when the latter's term of ten years had come to an end. The village elderman or *chôkata* was charged with the edition of the Church calendar, and a number of announcers or *kikiyaku* were to announce the weekly feasts, the days of fast and abstinence and other such matters.

Even St. Francis Xavier had urged the Japanese Christians to memorize the principal prayers, as for instance the Our Father, the Hail Mary, the Sign of the Cross, the Apostles' Creed, the Ten Commandments, the Salve Regina, the Confiteor and the fifteen Mysteries of the Rosary. As a matter of fact, the crypto-Christians who presented themselves to the French missionaries when Japan was again open to foreigners know these prayers very well and showed the Fathers numerous manuscript

195

copies of them.

Even doctrinal treatises sometimes were memorized and transmitted to later generations. In 1591 or 1592 the Jesuits had printed a short *Doctrina* in ten chapters, which enjoyed extraordinary popularity and was memorized by many. Father Raguet of the Paris Foreign Missions took the text down from the oral tradition of the small island of Ikitsuki, near Hirado, which in its entirety had preserved the faith, and subsequently published it in 1892. It tallies almost verbatim with the printed text of the *Doctrina* of 1592, except that an additional chapter, the 10th, on the Holy Eucharist, had been inserted.

Of the printed books published by the Jesuits between 1591 and 1611, almost nothing escaped the hands of the persecutors and no single printed copy was found among the crypto-Christians. The most important of all of them, however, *A Treatise on Contrition,* was available through many manuscript copies, as was discovered by the new missionaries. These poor Christians, being deprived of confession, the Holy Eucharist, Extreme Unction and all other sacraments except baptism, had to rely on perfect contrition as the only accessible means for a happy death. That the treatise served this purpose well is seen from the fact that it was copied so many times.

Holy pictures, medals, crosses, rosaries, statues

and other objects of piety were guarded by the crypto-Christians carefully as priceless treasures and were an additional help in the preservation of the faith. These, however, had to be carefully hidden from the eyes of the watchful police and were time and again seized by the raiders. To meet this danger, the Christians used statues of the Buddhist Goddess of Mercy, Kwannon, as substitutes for images of the Blessed Virgin, there being at least an outward resemblance. Since it was clearly a Buddhist deity it in no way could arouse the suspicion of the police, and for this reason a great many Maria-Kwannon have come down to us.

In this way the seed sown by St. Francis Xavier was never entirely eradicated. The faith had struck such deep roots in the hearts of the Japanese people that it could not be entirely destroyed even by the violent persecutions of more than two centuries and a half.

Raids upon the Crypto-Christians

We have seen that as late as 1697 great numbers of Christians were put to death because of their faith. Since, at the beginning of the 18th century, Father Sidotti was neither killed nor even tortured, one might believe that the violence of the persecution had abated to a certain extent, yet this conclusion is not altogether justified. Father Sidotti owed his lenient treatment undoubtedly to Arai Haku-seki's sense of fairness, yet he was, nevertheless, interned for years and finally met a martyr's death when he attempted to make converts. That we have no lists of martyrs after the beginning of the 18th century may be explained by the fact that all Christians submitted outwardly to the laws and professed a Buddhist sect.

It is certain that the descendents of Christians were always closely watched, had to stamp on the sacred pictures and were, moreover, periodically raided and thrown into jail, particularly the Christians of Urakami. This happened in 1790 and 1791, 1842 and 1856 at Urakami and from 1805 to 1807 in the Amakusa Archipelago. The French missionaries learned from the Urakami Christians that, in 1858,30 of their brethren had been incarcerated and tortured for two years. Twelve died in jail and the other 18, who were subsequently set free, very soon died as a result of the hardships and tortures endured during their long captivity.

In 1865 a Japanese teacher reported to Father Petitjean and Father Laucaigne that, about three years before, three or four persons had been cited before the governor of Nagasaki because they were suspected of being Christians. Their religious books were confiscated and handed over to a learn-ed bonze for examination. Although the kindhearted scholar recognized them clearly as Christian writings, he declared that they contained nothing but Buddhist doctrines, because he wanted to prevent bloodshed. One of the accused was, nevertheless, put to death. Thus, even eight years after the opening of Japanese ports, Christian blood was still being shed.

XI

Restoration of the Japanese Mission

Japan Not Forgotten by the Church

Father Sidotti's adventure was indeed the last attempt on the part of the Church to penetrate into closed Japan, but this does not mean that she had forgotten the abandoned flock of that country. Father Sidotti's heroism had aroused new interest in the Japanese mission in the Philippines, and, since as far as news had seeped through, it seemed that he had not been killed or even subjected to the torture, it was the general belief that the fury of the persecution had abated. The Franciscans were most eager to resume work in the country where so many of their brethren had died as martyrs. We do not know whether they took positive steps in this direction, but we do know that the Japanese grammer which the Franciscan Melchior Oyanguren published in Mexico in 1738 was meant to serve his brethren for the study of Japanese.

Father Gottfried Laimbeckhoven, Jesuit Visitor of the Chinese mission and after 1752 Vicar Apostolic of Nanking, was also planning the resumption of missionary work in Japan. He sent a courageous man, the father of a Chinese Christian, to investigate the situation of Christianity in Japan. After his return he reported that the coastal guards were extremely meticulous. The searching of incoming vessels was so thorough that a foreign priest could not possibly smuggle himself into the country. Smuggling in a Spaniard was prohibited under death penalty.

In 1832 the Paris Foreign Mission Society was charged with the evangelization of Korea and was simultaneously to take care of Japan as well. Although it was soon found that nothing could be done for the Christians in that country, the Holy See, nevertheless, took positive steps to receive information concerning conditions in Japan through its Dutch representatives. Thereupon the Vicar Apostolic of Batavia learned from a Dutch diplomatic agent who had spent many years in Japan that the rumors, according to which foreigners arriving in that country were requested to step on sacred pictures, were pure imagination. In any event, until the year 1884 neither the French missionaries nor the Holy See could do anything for the Christians in Japan.

Forcade in the Ryûkyûs

In 1844 the French minister to China, M. de Lagrené, succeeded in concluding a very favorable commercial treaty with that country. Simultaneously Contre-Admiral Cécille received orders to obtain similar results by peaceful negotiation from the adjacent countries of the Far East. Cécille devoted himself with great zeal to his mission and even resolved to approach the Japanese government with a treaty of commerce and friendship. He asked Father Libois, superior of the Paris Foreign Missions in Hongkong, to appoint a young priest as interpreter for his planned voyage to Japan. This Father was to study Japanese for some time in the Ryûkyû Islands and subsequently accompany him to Japan. Father Forcade was appointed to this post and on April 3, 1844, left Hongkong on the French warship *Alcmène* for the Ryûkyûs, where he arrived April 28. On the following day, which was the Solemnity of St. Joseph, he celebrated Mass for the first time in these islands.

Immediately after his arrival, Fornier-Duplan, commander of the *Alcmène*, began negotiating with the authorities to allow Father Forcade and his companion, Augustine Kô, a Korean Christian, to remain in the islands to study Japanese. It was a difficult and tedious negotiation which he attempted and, although he was treated with utmost courtesy, he was unable to obtain an answer. It was evident that the presence of foreigners was not desired. Instead of refusing Fornier-Duplan's request outright, the governor expressed his fears for Father Forcade's health if he were to remain in the islands. At last Fornier-Duplan simply decided to go. He left Father Forcade with his Korean companion at Naha, the capital, made the governor responsible for their lives and set sail to the great surprise and embarrassment of the officials.

It can be easily imagined that Father Forcade and Kô found themselves in no enviable situation. Outwardly they were treated with exaggerated courtesy, and were surrounded by a host of "helpful servants," who showed themselves eager to provide them with anything for which they might ask. As a matter of fact, however, these "friends" were nothing less than spies of the government; they were to watch all movements of the unwanted foreigners, who were indeed treated like prisoners. If they wished to walk outside their residence, they were told to avoid the busy roads leading to the city and to walk along the shore. They were accompanied by a host of secret service men. When they tried to speak to the peasants, the latter were driven away by the police, ordered to leave from the streets, to keep indoors, close the doors and windows and not speak to these foreigners. Forcade and Kô were never allowed to speak and much less to preach to the people, even if they had had sufficient command of the language to do so. They actually made but little real progress in Japanese. Sometimes they were even taught wrong expressions; they could not obtain books or teachers; and finally they were taught only literary Japanese, which was useless for their purpose.

Forcade, Vicar Apostolic of Japan

After a lapse of two years another French warship, the *Sabine,* visited the Ryûkyûs. It brought Father Turdu as Father Forcade's companion and a letter from his superior, Father Libois, to the effect that he had been appointed Vicar Apostolic of Japan. The *Sabine* was to remain only a short time in the Ryûkyûs, but its commander announced Cécille was on the way. Shortly after Cécille had dropped anchor at Naha, Father Forcade and Kô accompanied him to Nagasaki, where a commerical treaty with Japan was to be negotiated. The Japanese treated their unwelcome guests uncourteously and did not even allow anyone to land. Cécille's efforts under such conditions failed completely, and he soon left the inhospitable shores of Japan.

Forcade returned to Naha for a short time. Meanwhile a third missionary, Father Adnet, had arrived. On September 7, Forcade landed in Manila to receive episcopal consecration, but since this proved impossible, he left for Hongkong. There on February 21, 1847, he was consecrated Bishop. Seeing no possibility of entering his vicariate for the time being, he accepted the administration of the Hongkong vicariate as Pro-Vicar. Because of ill health he resigned from this office in 1852, returned to Europe and shortly after gave up his office of Vicar Apostolic of Japan. In 1853 he was appointed Bishop of La Guadalupe and in 1861 he was transferred to the diocese of Nevers. He became finally Archbishop of Aix in 1873 and died in 1885.

In Naha, Father Adnet had already died in 1848. Seeing that further stay in the Ryûkyûs was not only useless but even dangerous, Father Turdu in the same year left for Manila. Nothing had been accomplished at Naha, and the prospects for the opening of Japan looked very unpromising. Hence for the time being the Ryûkyû post was abandoned.

Commodore Perry Reopens Japan

The honor of opening Japan belongs to the people of the United States of America. On July 8,

Restoration of the Japanese Mission

1853, Commodore Perry appeared with a naval squadron in Edo Bay to present a letter of President Fillmore, in which he proposed to the *shôgun* a treaty of friendship and commerce between the two countries. The Japanese were greatly surprised, yet accepted the President's message, but in such a stiff and formal way that in less than half an hour the ceremony was over. Perry wisely did not expect an immediate answer but gave the shôgunate time to think the matter over and promised to return the coming year to receive the answer. He returned on February 11, 1854, and, to his satisfaction, a treaty of friendship and commerce was concluded. The two ports of Shimoda and Hakodate were to be opened to American ships. Subsequently Russia and England obtained similar treaties.

In 1855 the Paris missionaries resumed the post in the Ryûkyûs. One of the Fathers accompanied the French diplomat to Nagasaki as interpreter for the conclusion of a commercial treaty with the shôgunate, but for the time being no agreement was reached. Between 1856 and 1857 the Dutch were negotiating a similiar treaty. Among other things, they demanded freedom of worship for their people, the abolition of *efumi* and the admission of other nations, particularly the Portuguese. The treaty was concluded and, although *efumi* was at least abolished in name, the importation of religious books and pictures was explicitly prohibited. At last France also succeeded in concluding a treaty and was granted a number of noteworthy concessions, viz., freedom of worship for French citizens with the right to build churches and chapels, to lay out cemeteries, and all anti-Christian practices, particularly *efumi,* were abolished. It was due to the efforts of the American Consul General Townsend Harris that these concessions were made. The French treaty was ratified on September 22, 1859.

First Missionaries in Japan

In 1859 Father Girard was offered the office of Vicar Apostolic of Japan, but as he declined he was appointed administrator of the vicariate of Japan. During the same year he accompanied the French diplomat Duchesne de Bellecourt to Edo. Towards the end of 1859 Father Mermet established himself at Hakodate, where on January 5, 1860, he opened a modest chapel, the first Christian house of worship in Japan since 1614. In his optimism he, moreover, started a French school and even a kind of hospital. His hopes were not only not realized but he was also soon compelled to leave the city because of ill health.

At Yokohama Father Mounicou dedicated a church on January 12, 1862, on which occasion he also preached to the many Japanese visitors. Thereupon 55 Japanese were arrested by the police, and only when Father Mounicou promised to preach no more in Japanese were they released. Thus for the time being nothing could be done to make converts.

At the beginning of 1863 Father Furet took up residence at Nagasaki and was very soon joined by Father Petitjean, who the year before had left the Ryûkyûs, this hopeless outpost having been definitely abandoned. When Father Furet shortly after left for Europe, he was replaced by Father Laucaigne. On the slope of Ôura Hill, Father Petitjean built a church which was dedicated on February 19, 1865. No Japanese attended the ceremony, since it had been prohibited by the police. Thus it was impossible to approach the people, and the new church was usually locked. Father Petitjean, nevertheless, hoped to discover the descendents of the martyrs of old. Too, he believed that he had found the site of the martyrdom of the 26 saints who had died on February 5, 1597. His hopes were to be fulfilled beyond expectation only four weeks after the dedication of the new church.

Discovery of the Crypto-Christians

On March 17, Petitjean saw from the window of his room in front of the closed door of the church

The Catholic Church in Japan

a group of from 12 to 15 people, men, women and children, and was struck by their respectful demeanor, which seemed to indicate that it was more than curiosity that had attracted them to the church. A voice within him told Petitjean that he should go and meet these people. He went to the church, opened the door and entered. The Japanese followed him. In front of the altar the priest knelt down for a brief adoration, as he says himself: "I prayed to Our Lord Jesus Christ and confidently asked Him to give the right words into my mouth so as to move my hearers and win at least some of them for His love." Three middle-aged women approached him, knelt down beside him, and one of them, laying her hand on her breast, said to him in a whispered voice: "All of us have the same heart as you." "Indeed?" asked the astonished priest. "Where do you come from?" he asked. "We are all from Urakami, where nearly all have the same heart." Then one of the women asked: "Where is the statue of *Santa Maria?*" Instead of giving an answer Petitjean conducted the group to the altar of the Blessed Virgin, and all knelt down with him and wept for joy, exclaiming: "Yes this is indeed *Santa Maria!* Behold her divine Infant in her arms!"

Then they asked a lot of questions. One of the women remarked: "We celebrate the Feast of Our

Lord on the 25th day of the cold month. We were told that at midnight of that day He was born in a stable. Then He grew up to manhood in poverty and suffering to die for us on the cross in his 33rd year. At present we are in the season of sorrow. Have you also these feasts?"

"Yes," the priest answered, "we have today the 17th day of Lent." Then they spoke of St. Joseph, whom they called the foster father of Our Lord Jesus.

From that day on there came continually new visitors to the Ôura church so that the priests became alarmed lest the police might interfere and arrest the Christians. They therefore told them not to come again before the lapse of two weeks. The police had indeed always been extremely watchful, but both priests and Christians proceeded with such prudence and discretion, choosing for their interviews days of very bad weather or very early or late hours, that the police for a long time did not know what was going on. Petitjean, moreover, carefully guarded the secret of his great discovery from his foreign friends lest it be published in some Catholic paper abroad and thus come to the knowledge of the Japanese authorities. Very soon a priest went to visit the Christians at Urakami and instruct them. Their meetings took place mostly during night and in hidden places, in a garden, or among the bushes or in the mountains.

During the following months many more crypto-Christians were discovered. At the beginning of May a man came from the Gotô Islands to Nagasaki to see a doctor. He also visited the church and told the priest that he was a Christian and that his family had fled from Nagasaki to Gotô 200 years ago to escape persecution. He further stated that in the islands there were at least 1,000 Christians. Although he wanted to remain with the Fathers, they advised him to return home and receive first his father's permission. Full of joy he returned to Gotô and spread the good news that the *Bateren* (Fathers) had returned to Japan.

At Urakami about 1,300 Christians had soon contacted the priests, and about an equal number were discovered in the neighboring mountains. On May 15, 1865, Peter, the zealous baptizer of the island of Kaminoshima, came to see the church and the priests. He gave them a list of Christian communities in the neighborhood of Kaminoshima and moreover, maintained that there were Christians in nearly all parts of Japan, even close to Edo. In this, however, he was over-optimistic. Although Peter was convinced that the French priests were of the same kind as those who had converted his forefathers some 300 years before, he, nevertheless, wanted to know more about them to be absolutely sure. He therefore asked whether the Fathers acknowledged the "great chief of the Kingdom of Rome" and what was the name of the present pope? When he was told that he was called Pius IX and that he had sent the Fathers to Japan, he rejoiced extremely. Then he asked somewhat timidly: "Have you no children?" The answer was "You as well as your Christian and pagan brethren are the only children God has given us, for the priest must observe celibacy just as did your first missionaries". Overwhelmed with joy Peter exclaimed: "Oh, they are virgins, thanks be to God"! Now even the shadow of a doubt had disappeared that these priests were the legitimate successors of the *Bateren* of the early *Kirishitan* era.

In spite of all precaution the police grew suspicious and tried to find out whether the Fathers preached in public to the Japanese. They asked many questions about their religion, but nothing could be found which substantiated the charge that the priests acted against the law, although the bonzes and a host of spies had been mobilized to watch their dealings with the people. Thus in the beginning the police aquiesced, but it was not long before secret orders were issued to the effect that Japanese should not visit the church. Thereupon the Fathers kept the church locked during week days and received the visiting Christian leaders in their residence during night and early in the morning. Apart from this and occasional visits of the Fathers, four temporary "chapels" were soon opened at Urakami, which the priests visited during night to instruct the leading Christians, who in turn were to instruct those whom the priests could not visit, particularly women. Catechists began to visit far-off communities to instruct the people. They even discovered new Christians, as for instance in the Amakusa Archipelago and the islands in the neighborhood of Hirado. In the following year Christian centers were discovered at Imamura in the province of Chikugo, at Ômura and on Hirado Island.

Despite Father Petitjean's careful endeavor to keep his secret, it nevertheless seeped through. An account, full of errors, of the discovery of many Christians in Japan, appeared at the beginning of 1866 in the small Catholic paper *Le Rosier de Marie,* and filled Petitjean with great anxiety. Another source of fear was an order of his superior Father Furet, who meanwhile had returned from Europe, to again open the church to Japanese visitors. Still a third source of possible trouble, of a different kind, was Father Mounicou's catechism *Seikyô Yôri Mondô,* published at Yokohama in 1865. Petitjean had found a good number of manuscript prayers and doctrinal treatises among his Christians, written in the style of the *Kirishitan* era. The text was in Japanese, but the religious technical terms were the equivalents of the Latin or Portuguese words which had been used by the missionaries of old, written in the *kana* syllabary. While Father Petitjean was preparing a catechism in this style (on the basis of the old manuscripts), Father Mounicou published a catechism in the literary style of the kind used by the missionaries in China.

Father Girard, superior of the Japanese mission, gave Petitjean orders to use it for his flock and simultaneously sent him 30 copies. Petitjean, fearing that his Chrisitians might not only not understand the new terminology but also consider the contents of the book unorthodox since it was different in terminology from that they had inherited from their forefathers, appealed to Father Libois in Hongkong to ask Rome for a definite decision in such a delicate matter. Petitjean's appointment as Vicar Apostolic of Japan placed the decision into his own hands with the result that Mounicou's catechism was never used in Nagasaki. Father Petitjean was nominated Bishop and consecrated in Hongkong on October 21, 1866.

First Troubles with the Authorities

In 1866 a bonze asked for the governor of Naga-

saki's permission to build a new temple at Urakami,
and it was as good as certain that the Christians
would be urged to contribute, yet they were resolved to refuse. Because of a poor crop the governor
did not comply with the request and the cause of
conflict disappeared.

On November 20, 1866, the 30 leading Christians
of Urakami were summoned to the mayor. Two
bonzes had treacherously asked for instruction and
reported to the authorities that despite strict prohibition the Fathers had preached to the Japanese.
The 30 Christians, realizing the danger, asked
Father Laucaigne what they should answer and
were told to speak freely and firmly. The mayor
simply gave a fatherly warning to the Christians
not to visit the church henceforth. He did not ask
any questions and dismissed them without punishment.

During the next six months all was quiet so
that it was even possible to send a priest to the
Gotô Archipelago to instruct the Christians. As has
been stated above, during the persecution the Christians had finally submitted externally to the law
and registered as adherents of Buddhist sects. As
a result, their dead were buried by the bonzes, but
afterwards the Christians would often exhume their
dead and bury them according to Christian rite.
Having been instructed by the missionaries that

even outward adherence to Buddhism was not permissible for a Christian, they were resolved to call no more bonzes for the burial of their dead. It was easy to see that this would entail trouble, and it did.

On April 10, 1867, the mayor of Urakami gave strict orders that bodies which had been buried without the assistance of the bonzes should be exhumed. About the same time, the relatives of a deceased Christian refused to accept the services of the bonzes and declared, moreover, that they would have nothing at all to do with them. Thereupon the mayor of Urakami asked for a list of the Christians, which he would present to the governor of Nagasaki, and promised to speak in their favor. The governor dispensed them from the law and all was quiet again.

XII

More Persecution

Raids and Arrests

The governor of Nagasaki having made a great concession in favor of the Christians, the missionaries continued to visit and instruct the Christians of Urakami. In the Gotô Islands also missionary work was vigorously pushed. Not only could a priest reside there, but four temporary chapels were erected, where the Christians could meet and be instructed by the priest. The French minister had asked the *shôgun* to grant freedom of worship and the latter seemed willing to comply with his request. When on June 2, 1867, the statue of the Blessed Virgin in front of the Ôura Church was solemnly dedicated, even the vice-governor of Nagasaki was seen among the foreign diplomats who attended the ceremony. Thus the future of the Church looked very promising, but only for a time.

219

The Catholic Church in Japan

On July 14, only six weeks after the dedication ceremony, an armed band invaded one of the four Urakami chapels, plundered everything, maltreated, tied and arrested the proprietors and deported them to the Nagasaki prison. The same happened to the other three chapels, and all four of them were later destroyed. Sixty-three persons in all were arrested and jailed. The real cause of the raid was the still unsolved problem of the Buddhist funeral. At the same time 100 Christians were incarcerated at Ômura and treated very cruelly. Subsequently more Christians who had refused to call the bonzes to bury their dead were arrested at Urakami.

The 63 first prisoners were urged to apostatize, were chained and thus led through the city, suffered various kinds of tortures and starvation with the result that in the end all of them, except the catechist Dominic Zenyemon, grew weak and outwardly apostatized. By the good offices of the French minister the shôgunate promised to release these Urakami prisoners, but they were released only after they had apostatized. Having returned home, they revoked their apostacy and, as a result, were surrounded with guards, who, however, were soon withdrawn through the good offices of the French minister. The 110 Ômura prisoners were not released but treated with greater cruelty, whereas in the Gotô islands the Christians were left unmolested. During the coming months the *shôgun's* government abstained from further acts of violence, but the problem of the Buddhist funeral remained unsolved.

First Deportations

By the *coup d'etat* of January 3, 1868, the *shôgun* was declared deposed and the emperor reinstated into his legitimate rights. A new imperial governor was sent to Nagasaki. On March 16, he summoned to his palace 22 leading Christians, among them Dominic Zenyemon. All of them refused to give up their faith and were sent home with the advice to think the matter over. Five of the Ômura prisoners had managed to escape, but two were recaptured and cruelly tortured.

In April of the same year an imperial rescript was issued against the "detestable sect of the Christians" and on April 29, the heads of 184 Christian families were arrested and led to the governor of Nagasaki. They were urged to give up their faith, since the French intended to conquer Japan. All remained firm and were subsequently sent back to their homes. In vain the diplomats of France, England, Holland and Prussia asked the imperial government for a *dementi* of the wild anti-Christian rumors circulated far and wide.

The Catholic Church in Japan

On May 14, a new imperial rescript appeared against "the perverse Christian religion and all other perverse religions" and was posted on proclamation boards at the street corners. The "stubborn" were threatened with decapitation if heads of families, and with deportation if only dependents. When the foreign diplomats protested in the name of humanity, they were told that the Christians had violated the law and hence were to be punished.

On July 20, 114 Urakami Christians were called before the governor of Nagasaki, loaded on ships and deported to the districts of Tsuwano, Yamaguchi and Fukuyama. At Yokohama Bishop Petitjean again mobilized the foreign diplomats in behalf of his flock with the result that the deportation of the rest of the Urakami Christians was halted. Bishop Petitjean, moreover, managed to have ten candidates for the priesthood safely taken on a ship bound for Shanghai and brought to the college of Penang for the continuation of their studies. In November a violent persecution started in Gotô. Masses of Christians were arrested and most cruelly tortured. Nine of them were condemned to death. On January 3, 1868, of the 110 Ômura prisoners, 32 had died. At the beginning of 1869 there were from 400 to 500 Christians from Gotô, Ômura and other parts of the province of Hizen in jail.

When the foreign diplomats protested against the persecution in Gotô, they were told that Christians were no longer persecuted in these islands.

Height of the Persecutions

On January 1, 1870, 700 Urakami Christians were summoned before the governor of Nagasaki. Again the foreign diplomats, including the Englishman Sir Harry Parkes, endeavored to mediate and suspend the planned deportation, but all was in vain. From January 5 to 8, all Urakami Christians, 3,290 persons in all, were deported to various provinces of the empire. The foreign diplomats were told that the Christians were prosecuted as rebels, but Sir Harry Parkes did not admit the validity of this charge. The most that the Japanese government was ready to grant in view of the protests of the diplomats was the commutation of the death penalty into deportation. The remaining Christians in the neighborhood of Nagasaki were not molested and even managed to keep in contact with the Fathers. The United States minister, Long, made a last attempt to have freedom of worship granted by the Japanese government, but his efforts failed.

In December, 1871, a Japanese embassy headed by Prince Iwakura Tomomi started for the United States and Europe. It was accompanied by Minister Long to Washington. Four days before the departure of the embassy 60 Christian heads of families of the neighborhood of Nagasaki had been deported, which aroused a storm of indignation in the foreign press in Japan and abroad. The English Protestants, whose sympathy and indignation Sir Harry Parkes had aroused by his report on the persecution in Japan, demanded of Lord Granville energetic action in favor of the harassed Christians. These protests were not altogether in vain, for no further Christians were deported and those exiled in December, 1871, were repatriated in February, 1872. Even a number of the Urakami deportees, mostly apostates however, were sent back home during the next six months.

The Japanese embassy of Prince Iwakura was received rather coldly in America and Europe because of the persecution in their country, and a real campaign was undertaken by the press of various countries to denounce the policy of the Japanese government so as to force it to stop such barbaric action. In France, Léon Pagès published his memoir, *La persécution des Chrétiens au Japon et l'ambassade Japonaise en Europe,* for the French national assembly. The reporter for the French colonies, Desbassayns de Richemont, strongly pleaded the cause of the Japanese Christians in the same assembly, and the answer of M. de

More Persecution

Rémusat was animated by the same spirit. The same subject was taken up very sympathetically in England, Belgium, Germany and Italy. In England, the *Westminster Gazette* organized a national subscription so as to compel the English government to take energetic steps for the deliverance of the Japanese Christians. When in Brussels the Japanese embassy was led in procession through the city the population demanded clamorously the end of persecution in their country. The various cabinets of Europe urged the embassy in the same direction, pointing out that freedom of worship was the first prerequisite of a nation which claimed to be enlightened and cultured. These pleadings and protests did not fail to impress the embassy, which indeed urged their government to stop persecuting the Christians.

The End of Persecutions

The appeal of the Iwakuni embassy was heeded by the government of their country. In January, 1873, Bishop Petitjean could write to Europe that the exiled Christians were granted greater liberty and a more humane treatment. When towards the end of the same month the pleadings of Richmont and Rémusat in the French parliament became known in Japan, the imperial government assured the foreign diplomats that the deportees would be repatriated. The first semi-official declaration in this respect was made to the Italian minister on February 21, and a similar dispatch of the French minister is dated February 24. About that time the notices of prohibition of the Christian religion were removed from the street corners. The foreign press, nevertheless, took these semi-official declarations with great reserve, if not with suspicion. Finally on March 14, 1873, the imperial government issued an official declaration that the deported Christians would be repatriated, and Bishop Petitjean sent a telegram on April 7 to the effect that the anti-Christian notices had been removed and that the exiled Christians were being released. On the same day the first group of them returned to Urakami, and on April 27 the number of repatriated had risen to 671. By the end of May the last group arrived at Urakami.

The total number of exiled had amounted to 3,404 persons. Of these 660 had died. Five hundred had apostatized under the pressure of torture, ill treatment and starvation, but nearly all of them asked to be readmitted into the Church after their return. The exiles had been distributed over more than 20 provinces, from Satsuma in the extreme south of Kyûshû, to Etchû in the north of Hondo. Since the main object of the deportation had been to make apostates, the Christians were treated with extreme rigor, but in Satsuma, Tosa Iyo and, above all, in Ise they were the accorded more humane treatment.

Even at the time of their deportation the Christians had belonged to the poorer classes, but when they returned, they found themselves reduced to the utmost poverty, for in most cases their land had been seized by their pagan neighbors, and many of those who were able to recover it with the help of the government were compelled to sell it for a nominal price because of extreme poverty. As a result, the Christians had to turn to the poorer land in the mountains which was still available and for many years were among the poorest of the poor. Hastily constructed barracks, erected with the assistance of the government, provided temporary housing for the great number of homeless.

The crypto-Christians in touch with the priests numbered about 14,000 at the end of the persecution, and new communities were discovered from time to time during the following years. Not all of those who considered themselves Christians wanted to get in touch with the priests, partly because of the prospect of being deported, partly because their church elders were unwilling to hand over their influential position to the missionaries. These separated Christians are called *hanare* (the separated). They are found in many places in

The Catholic Church in Japan

greater or lesser numbers, but are most numerous in the island of Ikitsuki near Hirado. Of the 10,000 inhabitants there are only about 300 Catholics and the rest, with the exception of a handful of pagans, are *hanare*.

XIII

Recent History of the Japanese Mission

The Establishment of a Regular Hierarchy

Apart from the two earliest missions at Hakodate and Yokohama other stations had been established in Kôbe, Ôsaka and Niigata even before the end of the Meiji persecution, but for the time being it was impossible to do anything for the pagan Japanese. A good many years were to pass before the first baptisms were administered in these new churches. After the storm of persecution had subsided, however, a few converts were made outside the old Christian centers of Kyûshû and, as a result, Bishop Petitjean took steps for the division of his enormous vicariate, which embraced all of Japan. In 1876 it was divided into the vicariates of Northern and Southern Japan. Southern Japan, with its metropolis of Ôsaka, Bishop Petitjean kept for himself, and in the following year Monsignor Pierre

The Catholic Church in Japan

Osouf was appointed Vicar Apostolic of Northern Japan. Bishop Petitjean resided in Ôsaka, Bishop Osouf in the beginning at Yokohama, as Tôkyô had not as yet been opened to foreign residents.

In Northern Japan there were as yet hardly any Catholics, and in 1878 they numbered no more than 1,235. In the same year foreigners were permitted to reside in Tôkyô and, as a result, Bishop Osouf moved from Yokohama to the capital. Slowly the number of Catholics increased and several small communities were established in various cities. From Yokohama the missionaries made apostolic excursions to the neighboring districts and founded a number of tiny congregations. From 1878 on it became easier for foreigners to travel in the country and consequently the missionaries could move with greater ease and gather a larger crop. In this way small Christian communities were established at Sendai, Morioka, Ebisu on Sado Island, Sakata, Matsumine, Wakamatsu and Yamagata. Even in the barren field of Niigata, 63 baptisms were administered in 1878, and in Hakodate, 83 in the same year. From Tôkyô and Yokohama all larger cities in southwestern Japan were visited as far as Gifu, and in nearly all of them small Christian communities were erected.

By far the greatest number of Catholics in the vicariate of Southern Japan lived in the neighborhood of Nagasaki. At Urakami there were 3,750, in the islands around Nagasaki 2,000, in Hirado and the adjacent islands about 1,000, at Imamura in the province of Chikugo 1,200, in the Amakusa Archipelago 275. In Bungo, where Christianity had florished during the *Kirishitan* era, no crypto-Christians were discovered, and the foundation of the first missions in 1882 met with violent opposition and strong protest on the part of the pagans. In the larger cities of central Japan missions were opened, but the number of Christians remained very small for many years particularly in Kôbe, Ôsaka, Kyôto and Hiroshima. As a result, Bishop Petitjean changed his residence from Ôsaka to Nagasaki, where the bulk of his flock was concentrated. In 1884 Southern Japan numbered 24,656 Catholics.

Although Christianity had not been directly persecuted since the repatriation of the Urakami Christians in 1873, freedom of conscience had not yet been granted, and Christianity was merely tolerated. Buddhism and *Shintô* were the only religions which the government officially acknowledged and positively aided and protected. Since 1884 the press had advocated complete freedom of worship and the abolition of the privileges enjoyed by Buddhism and *Shintô*. These were withdrawn on August 12 of the same year. Less than two months later, on October 7, 1884, Bishop Petitjean died. He was succeeded by his auxiliary colleague Bishop Laucaigne, who died less than six months later on January 19, 1885. The new constitution promulgated on February 11, 1889, granted complete freedom of worship, and thus all barriers to Christian propaganda were definitely removed.

The first tangible result of freedom of conscience was a synod of the ordinaries of both Japan and Korea in March, 1890. It was held at Nagasaki on the 25th anniversary of the discovery of the Urakami Christians. It began with a large pilgrimage procession from Urakami to the Ôura Church on March 17. Subsequently processions from other Christian centers made their pilgrimages to Ôura. Neither the press nor the police showed the least sign of hostility.

In 1888 Southern Japan had been divided into the two vicariates of Ôsaka, Western Hondo and Shikoku; and Nagasaki and Kyûshû. In April, 1891, Northern Japan was split into the vicariates of Tôkyô, officially still named "Northern Japan," and Hakodate. During the same year Pope Leo XIII established a Japanese hierarchy with Tôkyô as metropolis, to which the suffragan bishops of Hakodate, Ôsaka and Nagasaki were subordinated.

Recent History of the Japanese Mission

Sisterhoods in the Service of the Mission

Even before the end of the Meiji persecution the Dames of St. Maure had arrived in Japan. At first they established themselves at Yokohama, where they opened a school, an orphan asylum and a hospital. Somewhat later they founded a home for the aged and another orphan asylum in Tôkyô. In 1877 the Sisters of the Holy Infant of Chaufailles established an orphan asylum in Kôbe and two years later a second one in Ôsaka, where, however, they met with violent opposition. In 1880 they founded at Nagasaki a school, an orphan asylum, a working home and a novitiate. In 1878 the Sisters of St. Paul de Chartres established themselves at Hakodate, where they opened a dispensary for the poor, a work home and a school for the catechetical instruction of children. In 1881 they began to work in Tôkyô.

Training of a Native Clergy

Faithful to their principle of considering the training of a native clergy their most important task, the priests of the Paris Foreign Mission Society from the outset had left nothing untried to recruit Japanese candidates for the priesthood. This was easily possible, because they had a Christian community which for 300 years had preserved

the faith amidst the most awful trials. Bishop
Petitjean therefore, soon after the discovery of the
Urakami Christians, employed a number of talented
boys as his "servants" so as to instruct them better
in Christian doctrine and prepare them for the
priesthood. In the same year, 1865, Father Cousin
began to teach Latin to these and and a couple
of other boys. Very soon six of them wanted to
become priests.

When the 1868 persecution broke out ten of these
boys, as we have seen, were sent to the college of
Penang to continue their studies unharassed. In
1870, 13 more students went with Father Laucaigne to Hongkong for the same purpose. After the
persecution most of these seminarians returned to
Japan to finish their curriculum. Of the ten who
had been sent to Penang, four died there; of the
remaining six, three had to interrupt or give up
their studies for various reasons, and the remaining
three were ordanied priests on December 31, 1882.

For a number of years Nagasaki, Tôkyô and
Ôsaka each had its own seminary, but since Nagasaki alone had a sufficient number of candidates,
after 1890 all ordinaries sent their students to the
seminary of Nagasaki, which thereby became the
regional seminary for all of Japan. Up to 1894, 23
Japanese candidates were raised to the priesthood.

234

Recent History of the Japanese Mission

The Catholic Press

Immediately after the discovery of the Urakami Christians, Bishop Petitjean had begun the compilation of catechisms, prayer books and devotional pamphlets as well as the publication of a Church calendar. Simultaneously Father Mounicou had edited and published a catechism at Yokohama before a single Japanese had asked for instruction. As we have seen Bishop Petitjean was afraid that the unaccustomed terminology of Father Mouncou's book would scandalize the Nagasaki Christians, who were accustomed to the *Kirishitan* terminology, and so he did not distribute the Yokohama catechism but doubled his efforts to bring out a Christian doctrine in the ancient style. The first printed edition appeared in 1868 under the title *Seikyô Shogku Yôri* (Fundamentals of Christian Doctrine). In the same year he published a prayer book *Seikyô Nikka* (Daily Prayers of a Christian) and a Church calender.

Bishop Petitjean was well aware that in the 16th and 17th centuries the Jesuits and the friars had printed many works in Japanese and so he began to search for such books in Manila, Macao, Rome and Portugal. In Manila he found a book on the rosary, a book of meditations, two dictionaries and two grammars; in Rome, a book on confession, a catechism and a copy of the Latin-

The Catholic Church in Japan

Portuguese-Japanese dictionary which the Jesuits
had printed in Amakusa in 1595. The book on the
rosary, extracts from the book of mediations, the
treatise on confession as well as a pamphlet on
contrition, which he had discovered among his
Christians, he republished in Shanghai during the
years of persecution, and a new edition of the Amakusa dictionary he issued in Rome. Simultaneously a number of other devotional and apologetical
pamphlets were printed during the persecution in
Shanghai and later in Japan.

All of these books with the exception of the
Amakusa dictionary were woodblock or litho-
graphic prints, since at that time movable type was
scarcely used in China and Japan. All were written in *Kirishitan* style, and in 1875 Bishop Petitjean
gave his *imprimatur* for a new catechism in Chinese style. From then on books in this as well
as in *Kirishitan* style appeared simultaneously,
some of them with Bishop Petitjean's *imprimatur*.
After 1883, however, works in *Kirishitan* style
were no longer published. After 1877 nearly all
books of the mission were printed with movable
metal type, which by that time had become the
ordinary method in Japan. Up to 1880 the Paris
missionaries had published about 50 books and
pamphlets.

In 1881 the first Catholic monthly review,

Kôkyô Banpô, appeared. From 1885 to 1888 its title was changed to *Tenshu no Bampei* and for the following four years to *Kôkyô Zasshi,* after which time it was discontinued. In 1892 a new review, *Koe (Vox Catholica),* was started. It still appears under the same name. Apart from these periodicals a number of others, some in Latin for the benefit of the missionaries, appeared during the nineties and the following decades. Two scientific reviews on Japanology deserve to be mentioned, namely, *Mélanges Japonais* (1904-1910) by the priests of the Paris Foreign Mission Society, and *Monumenta Nipponica* (1938-1943 and 1951 to the present day) by the Jesuit Fathers of Sophia University, Tôkyô.

Charities

We have seen already how all three sisterhoods, devoting themselves to the Japanese mission, from the outset gave themselves to charitable works. They moreover nursed poor patients in their homes or received them into their hospitals. During epidemics Catholic sisters aroused the admiration of the pagans by their heroic devotion to the victims of the plague. This happened during the cholera epidemcis in 1886 and 1890, and during the influenza plague in 1890 and 1891. Native Japanese sisters in Nagasaki and surroundings did wonders of charity during the cholera plague in 1890 and engaged in various other works of charity, particularly for abandoned children. In 1888 the first leper asylum was founded at Kôyama, at the foot of Mount Fuji, by Father Testvuide, who had corresponded with Father Damian of Molokai and took advice from him concerning the treatment of lepers. During the following decades the number of Catholic hospitals and charitable institutions grew continually so that today there are no less than 137 in Japan.

Education

From the beginning, priests and sisters had established parochial schools for the elementary education of the children of Catholics, but since education was more and more monopolized by the government it became very difficult and in many cases impossible to maintain these schools, for they had to comply with government regulations and standards to receive recognition. On the other hand the public schools, particularly middle schools, presented no small danger to Catholic students, and so the erection of Catholic secondary schools seemed an absolute necessity.

In 1887 Bishop Osouf invited the Marianists to Tôkyô to establish a middle school for boys. It was opened in the following year. In 1892 a similar institution was erected at Nagasaki and a higher commercial school in Ôsaka. A fourth school was opened at Yokohama in 1901 for boys of foreigners and for Eurasians.

Simultaneously the schools of the various sisterhoods managed to secure government charters for primary and secondary education. Up to 1912 the Dames of St. Maure established girls' elementary and high schools in Yokohama, Tôkyô and Shizuoka. The Sisters of St. Paul de Chartres opened schools of the same type at Hakodate, Tôkyô, Sendai, Morioka and Yatsushiro, and the Sisters of the Holy Infant of Chaufailles had girls' schools at Urakami. In 1908 the Madames of the Sacred Heart opened a girls' elementary and high school in Tôkyô, and in 1909 the Sisters of the Holy Ghost started a girls' high school at Akita.

Although primary and secondary education, especially of girls, was making good progress, there was not a single Catholic university in Japan, whereas Protestants had paid great attention to university education from the very beginning. To make up for this deficiency in Catholic education, Pope Pius X ordered the Society of Jesus to open a Catholic university in the capital of the empire. In 1908 the first Fathers arrived in Japan, and in 1913 they succeeded in founding Sophia University (Jôchi Daigaku) in Kôjimachi Ward in Tôkyô.

The Catholic Church in Japan

The number of Catholic schools, particularly girls' high schools, greatly increased during the following decades, and after the end the Second World War the number of Catholic institutions increased by leaps and bounds. Today Catholics have 25 elementary and 60 middle and high schools, 15 junior colleges and six universities.

Summary of Events from 1891 to 1945

In 1895, the second synod of the ordinaries of Japan was held in Tôkyô. In 1897, the 300th anniversary of the 26 holy martyrs was celebrated with great solemnity at Nagasaki.

Until 1904 the priests of the Paris Foreign Mission Society were the only missionaries in Japan, but during the subsequent decades many missionary societies were given a share in the work of evangelization. In 1904 Spanish Dominicans were entrusted with the new prefecture apostolic of Shikoku, the German Fathers of the Society of the Divine Word received the prefecture apostolic of Niigata in 1912, and of Nagoya in 1922. Sapporo with the greater part of Hokkaido was transferred to German Franciscans in 1915 and Hiroshima with the five western prefectures of the mainland of Honshû to German Jesuits in 1923. Canadian Franciscans were given Kagoshima prefecture with the Ryûkyûs in 1925, and Italian Salesians, Miyazaki with a part of Kyûshû in 1928.

In 1927 the first native bishop, Januarius Haya-
saka, was consecrated by Pope Pius XI and entrusted with the new diocese of Nagasaki which
comprised the civil prefecture of that city. The
rest of the former diocese of Nagasaki remained
as the diocese of Fukuoka under the jurisdiction
of the Paris Foreign Mission Society. In 1937 a
new prefecture apostolic of Kyôto was detached
from the diocese of Ôsaka and entrusted to the
American Maryknoll Society. The diocese of
Hakodate had been taken over by Canadian Dominicans in 1931. In 1936 it was renamed after the
more central city of Sendai, and in 1951 the district of Hakodate was transferred to the Vicariate
Apostolic of Sapporo.

Ten years after the consecration of the first
native bishop, the archdiocese of Tôkyô received
also a Japanese Metropolitan in the person of
Archbishop Doi. Archbishop Chambon received
the new diocese of Yokohama, the larger part of
the former archdiocese of Tôkyô, which henceforth comprised only the Tôkyô and Chiba prefectures. From the Yokohama diocese a new prefecture apostolic was detached in 1939 for the
Canadian Franciscans, who had to be replaced by
the Japanese secular clergy in Kagoshima and the
Ryûkyûs.

The Catholic Church in Japan

In 1891 the number of Catholics in Japan amounted to 44,505, of whom 27,909 lived in Kyûshû. In the same year the archdiocese of Tôkyô had a Catholic population of 9,660 souls. In 1900 there were 55,091 Catholics in Japan, but the archdiocese of Tôkyô had even a little less than in 1891. From 1891 until 1910 the arch-diocese of Tôkyô had increased only by 40 souls, whereas the Catholic population of Japan had risen from 44,505 to 65,107 souls. In Kyûshû, Catholics increased about 1,000 a year, but this was scarcely more than the natural increase, for there were very few baptisms of adults. From 1931 to 1941 the Catholic population increased from 96,323 to 121,-128, that is by about 2,500 every year. The small-est increase was in 1938, 1,631; the largest, 4,274 in 1939.

From these statistics it appears that the growth of the Catholic population was very modest indeed. While the statistics show a marked increase be-tween 1873 to 1891 this is due in the main to the fact that time and again old Christian centers were discovered, whereas the number of converts from paganism was never very great. One of the main reasons was the many misconceptions which for more than 250 years had seen in Christianity a menace to national independence and which were fostered by the flood of anti-Christian novels which had painted the religion of the West in the darkest and most fantastic colors.

When these prejudices had died down to a certain extent, the rising tide of nationalism set up a new barrier against Christianity. Another reason for the slight progress of the mission was the infiltration of Western unbelief and materialism. Competition of numberless Protestant sects and of Russian orthodoxy also worked against the Catholic missions.

With the outbreak of the Manchurian war in 1931 nationalism rose to fever pitch and Christianity was suspected more and more, particularly by the militarists. The situation was aggravated by the outbreak of the Chinese war in 1937 and particularly by the approach of the Second World War.

In 1932 the *Shintô* problem threatened for a time the very existence of Catholic schools and with them of the entire mission. The question was finally settled by an official declaration of the Ministry of Education to the effect that the ceremony demanded from students on visiting the *Shintô* shrines was nonreligious and merely an expression of patriotism. Thereupon Catholics were allowed to perform the ceremony, and this decision was confirmed by Rome.

For many years the government had proposed

The Catholic Church in Japan

a "Religions' Organization Bill", which was to bring all religions, Christianity included, under closer control of the state. Many times the bill was shelved, but shortly before the outbreak of the World War it passed the Diet. One of its main objects was to Japonicize the Christian churches and schools.

In the autumn of 1940 all foreign-born ordinaries tendered their resignations. Rome accepted the offer and appointed Japanese priests as administrators of all dioceses, vicariates and prefectures apostolic. Since then the Japanese hierarchy has been under native leadership.

At the outbreak of the last war the priests, brothers and sisters of the allied powers were interned and subsequently in part repatriated. As a result many parishes lost their pastors, and missionary propaganda came to a standstill.

After the autumn of 1944 the endless and almost daily air raids greatly added to the hardships and laid waste most of the churches and Catholic institutions. Tôkyô, Ôsaka, Kôbe, Nagoya, Okayama, Hiroshima and Nagasaki were hit hardest. In Nagasaki alone about 8,500 Catholics fell victims to the atomic bomb, so that the only large Catholic community which had survived the century-old persecution was almost wiped out. Only those who happened to be absent survived and now form

the nucleus of the greatly reduced flock of Urakami.
When finally on August 15, 1945, the Emperor announced on the radio that he had accepted the
conditions of surrender, Catholics were filled with
gratitude towards the Lord for having brought an
end to the tribulation.

Epilogue: Since the End of the War

If anywhere in the world, the Catholic Church
in Japan has been given a very large share in
the Cross of the Savior, which was to be also the
lot of His followers. The seed planted by St.
Francis Xavier had produced marvelous fruit,
which, however, was only too soon destroyed by
a persecution unparalleled in history. The heroic
testimony of the martyr Church of Japan will for-
ever be a glorious page in the history of this
generous nation. The fact that in spite of an un-
interrupted persecution of 250 years the faith was
preserved would seem to be unique in the annals
of the Catholic Church. The new persecution at
the beginning of the Meiji Restoration aroused the
indignation but also the admiration of the world
and finally compelled the persecutors to give in.
Even so the years from 1873 until 1945 were a
real Way of the Cross. Prejudices were many,
conversions few and the apparent freedom of conscience amounted to little more than a very pre-

The Catholic Church in Japan

carious truce. After the lapse of 70 years disaster again threatened to destroy all that had been accomplished under most extraordinary hardships.

Yet with the close of the war a new era has dawned for the harassed Church of the insular empire. At the beginning of the occupation the Religions' Organization Bill was suppressed and complete freedom of worship granted. The confiscated churches and institutions were returned, the demolished edifices rebuilt, and Christian propaganda started with new vigor and great enthusiasm. When at the beginning of 1946 the Emperor solemnly renounced all claims to religious worship the last obstacle to the adoption of the Christian religion was removed.

The shock of a lost war, the hardships and privations of the war and the post-war period had taught the Japanese people that they had entertained illusory hopes and striven after false ideals. As a result a very great many turned their eyes, amidst so much chaos and disappointment, towards Christianity to find solid ground to stand upon.

During the war there had been scarcely any conversions; after it the number of baptisms rose quite rapidly. In 1941 there had been 121,128 Catholics in Japan. In spite of the approximately 10,000 victims of the war, in 1948 the same figure was attained once more. In 1949 Catholics num-

bered 130,388; in 1950, 142,460; in 1951, 157,241; in September, 1952, 171,875; and in September, 1953, 185,284.

The pre-war missionary staff was in no way able to meet the greatly increased demand for instruction and to harvest the rich crop. As a result, the old missionary societies increased their staffs, and a great many new ones came to share their work. In 1941 there worked in Japan 445 priests (among them 136 Japanese), 234 brothers (132 Japanese) and 1,794 sisters, the majority of whom were natives. According to the Catholic Directory of 1951 there were 29 societies of men (priests and brothers) and 54 of women; 877 priests (195 Japanese); 271 brothers (169 Japanese) and 2,206 sisters (1,874 Japanese). According to the latest statistics (September 4, 1953): 1,048 priests (238 Japanese), 334 brothers (191 Japanese), 2,954 sisters (2,037 Japanese).

Simultaneously the number of Catholic schools, hospitals and charitable institutions has increased greatly since 1941, and the number of vocations to the priesthood and religious life shows a very marked increase. The work of reconstruction has met with extraordinary success, the disrupted economy has recovered and been stabilized and, above all, order and peace have been restored and maintained. As a result, the eyes of the entire world are today directed toward Japan, and the Catholics of all countries rightly expect a momentous growth of the Church in that land which has suffered so enormously for the faith and has populated heaven with a glorious army of martyrs. As was to be expected, the first rush to the Church in the post-war period has somewhat subsided, but even so, the number of baptisms is many times greater than it had been for more than 70 years, so that even the greatly increased missionary staff is unable to satisfy the many who ask for instruction. If anywhere, certainly in Japan Tertullian's famous words will be fulfilled to the letter: "The blood of the martyrs is the seed of Christianity."

INDEX

1. In Regno Figen in Civitate Nangasaqui Collegiu, Domon Probationis, Domu Misericordie, et Hospitale et interritorio Residentias Sex, et multas Ecclesias notata Signo +.

2. In Arima Civitate Collegium et Seminarium in ditions eius Residentias Septem, et multas Ecclesias

3. In Vomura Civitole Collegium et in ditione Residentias quinqs, et multas Ecclesias.

4. In Civit Firando Coluncho alia Resid 2, et multas Eccles.

5 In Insulis Goto Res. 2. et in Supraditis Eius vsus publicati eret concilium Tridentinam.

6. In Amausa Residet. et Eccl.as

7. In Regno Satcuma in Civit. Cangoxima Residet Eul.as

8. In Regno Fiunga Resid et Eu.

9 In Regno Fingoin Civ. Vto Colleg. et in ditisne Residentias decem et multas Ecclestas

10. In Regno Bungo in Civ. Usuqui Colleg In funai Domum Probat. et in ditione Resid quinqs et mult Eccl.as

11. In Regno Ciuunga Resid et aliques Ecclesias.

Regno Bugen in Civitate Cocura coll inchoatu et Resid

12. et Ecclesias

13 In Regno Chiunjen in Civ. Facata coll inchoatum. et Resid. 3 et Ecclesias

14. In Regno Nangate in Civ. Ximonoxequi Resid. et Ecclesias.

15. In Regno Suuo in Civit. Yamanguchi Res. et Eccl.as

16. In Regno Aqui in Civit. Firoxima Res. et Ecclesias

17. In Regno Bitchu Eccl.as

18. In Regno Bijen Ecclesias

19. In Regno Farima Resid. et Eulesias.

20. In Regno Tiunoacuni in Civ. Ozaca Resid et altera in Civit. Sacai.

21. In Regno Cauachi Eccles

22. In Regno Yamaxiro in Metropoli Miaco coll. et in eadem Resid et aliam in Civ. Fuximi et Ecclesias

23. In Regno Tamba Eccl.as

24. In Regno Vomin Civ. Anxuqui Resid et Seminariu

25. In Regno Vacasa Eccl.as

26. In Regno Xochijen Eccl.os

27. In Regno Canga in Civ. Canaxaue Res. et Ecclesias

28. In Regno Noto Ecclesias

29. In Regno Mino in Civ. Quifu Residet Ecclesias

30. In Regno Vouari in Civ. Quiyaiu Res. et Ecclesias

31. In Regno Suetiga Curia Imperatoris Daifu Resi et Ecclesias.

32. In Regno Mulaxi in Curia Yendo Imperatoris Xogui. Resid. et Ecclesias

33 In Regno Quinacuni Res Sidentiam et Ecclesias.

Pars cœce

OCCIDENS

IA
Noua
Per R.P.An
S
Ad

Ogui

Tajima P

Argenti fodina

Tango P

NIP

Tanbe 22 Yamaxi

23 20. Meaco Tiunoasua

Foquip

Yalugu

Thorcon

Imabe

Mino

P

Harima

Argans

fo aureidaumo

Bitchu

Iuami

P

Bigen P

Ocagama

Tomo

Aqui P

Suuo

P

Yaenamayu

Bungu P

Tamu

Vranda

35 Quinacuni P

Nanguta

14 + P

15 + P

Xinonan qui

Fosata

Cisacata

Yamanguchi

Tann

36 Iyo P

35 Aua P

Cataixu

XICOCO

Figen

Cluorjen

Bugen

Funai

Dongo

P Tosa

Yapu reximai

Oscia

Cato

Chicango

Yaranjunai

Simabara P

Nangasaqui

Amm

Arima

X. 6

VIC

Cunifred

Bungo P

Iappon de
Siue Regna
ta est Fides
Religioforu
tena Christia
Habuit Soci
Collegia fex
Collegia inc
tionis duas
ria duo Pl

Ulugui

Cangoxima

Satcu ma P

Tango P

Calixuira

Vofumi

Tiungo + P

MO 7

S Clara

Cocori + M

Tanegux

S. Franciscus Xauorius Iapponia Aptus appellit Cangoximam 15 Aug an 1543